BLIZZARD'S
OUTDOOR TOYS

Sterling Publishing Co., Inc.   New York

BLIZZARD'S
OUTDOOR TOYS

RICHARD BLIZZARD

ACKNOWLEDGEMENTS

The start of a new book for the BBC involves many enthusiastic people who advise, help, support and encourage me at all stages. A new book also involves making a TV series where the skills of many are required to show you how the toys are made. A sincere 'Thank you' is due to all these people for their patience with me all through this project.

The Book:
Peter Farley and Mervyn Hurford for all the work on producing the plans and the cutting lists. Jenny Spring and Mary Davis for 'braving' my handwriting and turning pages of untidy paper into typescript. The Fire Chief and his 'watches' at Stroud Fire Station for allowing us to photograph our fire engine there.

At BBC Books: Jennie Allen for asking many questions and sorting out all the various processes which turned the typescript into a book. (An author who has Jennie to help is assured success!); Bernie Cavender who designed the book, planned all the photographs and helped us all while we carried Trojan horses, castles and fire engines to different locations in Gloucestershire!; Suzanne Webber and Nicholas Chapman who kept a friendly eye on us all as things progressed.

The TV series:
Chris Stone, BBC Contracts, Bristol, for always being so helpful with all those bits of paper.

At BBC Pebble Mill Birmingham: Phil Thickett and 'Budget' who tackled the daunting task of producing and directing a Blizzard series; also Clare Chambers, Eileen Bayliss, Dave Brazier, Debbie Hood, Helen Smith and Roy Barratt, whose wonderful set design made me feel at home in a television studio; Mervyn Hurford who not only assisted me with bits and pieces on screen but who worked desperately hard behind the scenes to make things flow smoothly; Jim Dumighan who kept an eye on us all; and last, but by no means least, the sound, lighting and camera teams.

Suppliers:
Geoff Baldwin, David Prosser, John Spon-Smith, Marie Jennings and Chris Wollard of Stanley Tools; James Goodman of Leedex for supplying of Robert Bosch electrical tools; Jim Murray, Herbert Closterman, Norman Collier and Mike Lustig at AEG for the use of the electric screwdrivers. Bill Emmerich of Emmerich (Berlon) Ltd for supplying with two beautiful beech workbenches (they were almost too good to work on); Peter Grimsdale and Jack Baird of the Swedish Finnish Timber Council for all their advice and help in buying and using timber in the series; Hazelock ASL Ltd for the fire engine pumps; Mr and Mrs Davis and their team for storing and transporting all the toys so carefully.

And finally – thank you to Beth Campbell for introducing me to the wonderful word 'gribbly'. (Well, we all know what a gribbly hole looks like, don't we?)

The plans for the toys and models were drawn by Peter F Farley and Mervyn Hurford

The black and white and colour photographs were taken by Peter Pugh-Cook

The diagrams in the tools and techniques section were drawn by Alan Burton

The publishers would like to thank Stanley Tools and Robert Bosch for their assistance.

Library of Congress Cataloging-in-Publication Data

Blizzard, Richard E.
  [Outdoor toys]
  Blizzard's outdoor toys / Richard Blizzard.
    p. cm.
  "First published in the U.K. in 1988 by BBC Books"—T.p. verso.
  Includes index.
  ISBN 0-8069-6903-2
  I. Wooden toy making. 2. Outdoor recreation for children—Equipment and supplies. I. Title.
TT174.5.W6B578 1989   88-32446
684'.08—dc19   CIP

Copyright © 1988 by Richard Blizzard
Published in 1989 by Sterling Publishing Co. Inc.,
Two Park Avenue, New York, New York 10016
First published in the U.K. in 1988 by BBC Books, a division of BBC Enterprises, London
Manufactured in the United States of America
All rights reserved
ISBN 0-8069-6903-2

This book was set in 10 key on 11 point Gill by Rowland Phototypesetting Ltd, Bury St Edmunds, Suffolk, England

CONTENTS

Foreword   6

Periscope   7
Strength Tester   9
Swing   13
Slide   17
See-Saw   21
Market Stall   25
Viking Longboat   28
Dump Truck   32
Mail Truck   38
Volvo Shovel-Loader   43
Castle   53
Trojan Horse   65
Garden House   71
Fire Engine   75

Following the Plans   89
Tools and Techniques   90
Materials   95
Index   96

Throughout the book metric measurements are given first, followed by imperial measurements in brackets

FOREWORD

**By Jim Dumighan
BBC TV**

In some ways, rather like the Pied Piper of Hamelin, Richard Blizzard has a mesmeric effect on people. They seem to follow him in droves and, subsequently, learn much from the experience.

I discovered this in 1978 when, as Editor of BBC 1's lunchtime magazine programme – *Pebble Mill At One* – I first tried out this young, ebullient toy-maker from Gloucestershire, allowing him a handful of appearances, each lasting no more than six or seven minutes.

The viewers' verdict was swift and succinct; Richard Blizzard, a warm, natural communicator but an absolute beginner as a television performer, struck an instant chord, and people in their thousands clamoured for his homespun advice and his easily understood fact sheets to help them make cheap, but handsome wooden toys. In the ten years since then, Richard has turned the hobby of wooden toy-making into an international growth industry via his BBC television series and his publications.

During the war years with their inevitable shortages, thousands of youngsters were blissfully happy to receive a wooden toy at Christmas, which had been lovingly 'knocked together' by a Dad or an Uncle. Now, nearly 50 years on, Richard Blizzard has rekindled a new interest in attractive and sturdy wooden toys, reminding us all that they take only a little time, patience and enthusiasm to produce.

Working with and learning from Richard Blizzard is, as I have found out, lots of fun. He really is the Pied Piper with a plane in his hand.

PERISCOPE

The Knights of the Round Table would have appreciated this periscope to look over walls or around corners as an invaluable secret weapon when defending their castles.

It is advisable to buy your mirrors before starting any woodwork in case you can't obtain the exact size that I have used. I found that small mirror tiles were ideal for the job. Within reason, the tube can be as long as you like.

I Your first job, once you have chosen your mirrors, is to cut out the two corner blocks on which they must be mounted.

Take a length of timber, the thickness of the mirror's width, and mark out two right-angled triangles (see plans) on the side face making sure that the length of the diagonal is the same as the length of the mirrors. It helps if the timber is longer than you actually need for the two blocks in order to give you some 'elbow room'.

Fix one end of the timber firmly in a vice and, using a tenon saw, cut off the corner blocks. Remove saw cuts and double check that the mirrors fit on the diagonal faces.

2 Cut out the back and front of the periscope 'tube' from plywood. Glue the corner blocks on in the correct position (see plans).

3 Cut out the top and bottom of the 'tube' and glue and panel pin these in place.

4 Now glue your mirrors in position (you can use self-adhesive pads, if you like). When the glue has dried, glue and panel pin the sides on to form the tube. You will need to be fairly gentle at this stage to avoid cracking the mirrors.

5 To prolong the toy's life I would advise spending some time explaining to your children how the periscope works, and that the mirrors will break if it is dropped or roughly handled. Do be sure they understand that if a breakage does occur, they should call an adult to clear up the pieces of mirror rather than try to pick them up themselves. It might even be a good idea to fit handles on the tube for extra safety.

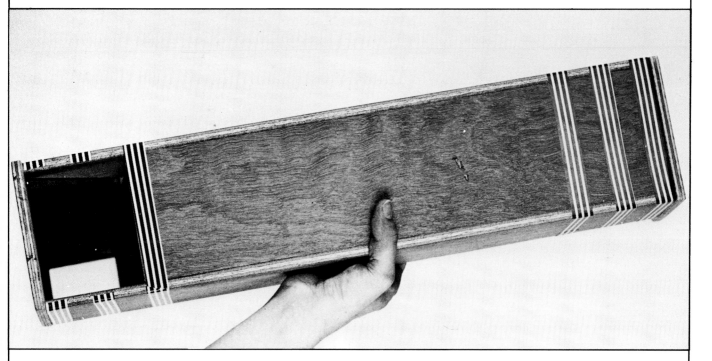

Cutting list

Side	2 off	552 × 108 × 9mm (21¾ × 4¼ × ⅜in)	Plywood
Front and rear	2 off	476 × 108 × 9mm (18¾ × 4¼ × ⅜in)	Plywood
Top and bottom	2 off	152 × 127 × 9mm (6 × 5 × ⅜in)	Plywood
Corner block	2 off	108 × 76 × 76mm (4¼ × 3 × 3in)	Timber

Ancillaries

	2 off	108mm (4¼in) mirror wall tiles	

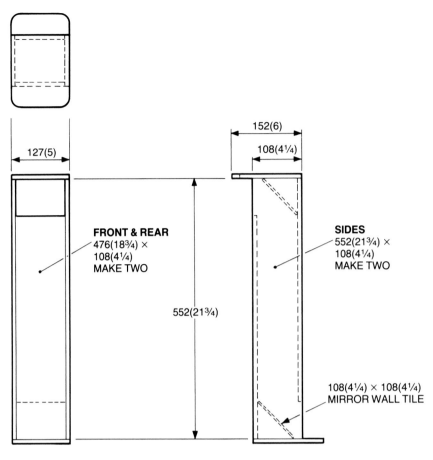

127(5)

152(6)

108(4¼)

FRONT & REAR
476(18¾) ×
108(4¼)
MAKE TWO

SIDES
552(21¾) ×
108(4¼)
MAKE TWO

552(21¾)

108(4¼) × 108(4¼)
MIRROR WALL TILE

GENERAL ARRANGEMENT
FABRICATED IN 9(⅜) THICK PLYWOOD

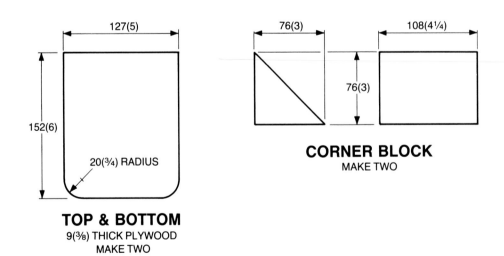

127(5)

76(3)

108(4¼)

152(6)

76(3)

20(¾) RADIUS

CORNER BLOCK
MAKE TWO

TOP & BOTTOM
9(⅜) THICK PLYWOOD
MAKE TWO

'Roll up! Roll up! Roll up! Test your strength on this mighty bicep-bulging machine! Only the strongest need apply – test your muscle power and stamina. Roll up! Roll up! Roll up!'

This toy is really just for fun, but it does provide a challenge for both boys *and* girls. After some initial testing, the children will learn that it is not all brute strength, since a certain knack can be acquired when hitting the target area which will literally rocket the disc to the top.

Before letting the children 'loose' on this toy, do explain how it works, and that if the mallet is not used sensibly then someone standing by could get hurt. Make sure that 'visiting' children understand the dangers of getting hit by the mallet or getting fingers pinched. If you don't feel certain your children will use it sensibly, only let them loose on it under supervision!

1 Start by making the base. This is made up of a lateral cross bar (i.e. the piece of timber which goes from side to side) and a fore-and-aft base cross member (i.e. one that crosses it at right angles). Where they join in the middle you need to cut a halving joint (see page 90) and also drill a hole right through to take the vertical pole.

When the cross bar and cross member are finished, glue them together Fix a screwed eye into the cross member as shown on the plans.

2 Cut out the two mounting blocks of wood needed for the front of the fore-and-aft cross member. Screw them together and then screw the bottom one to the cross member by passing screws up into the wood via the underside of the cross member. Make sure that these mounting blocks are screwed firmly in place as they will have to take a great deal of pounding when the toy is in use.

3 Now make the pivot beam.

i Cut out the three pieces of timber needed, the main one of which should be made of hardwood such as beech or ash to withstand all the thumping. Glue the smaller pieces of timber to either side of one end.

ii Cut out a disc of plywood for the target area. Glue and screw this firmly onto the wide end of the pivot beam assembly. Secure fixing here is vital as the disc takes all the impact of the mallet.

iii Attach the underside of the pivot beam to the top mounting block using a back flap hinge. Buy one that has plenty of fixing holes and a good stout knuckle joining the two halves together.

iv Now mark out the fork end of the pivot beam on to a piece of plywood. Use a jigsaw to cut out the curves and the slot. Pre-drill the holes for screws that will attach it to the pivot beam. Glasspaper the edges and then screw it in position.

v Fit a screwed eye to the underside of the end of the main pivot beam. Attach a piece of elastic (catapult elastic is best) to

this eye and attach the other end to the screwed eye in the fore-and-aft cross member.

vi Glue a thin rubber pad on to the top mounting block to absorb some of the shock.

4 Cut a piece of dowel rod to length for the vertical pole. Glue it in position in the base of the strength tester. Slide a length of plastic overflow pipe over the dowel rod – this will provide a smooth surface for the height-indicating disc to slide on.

5 Cut out the height-indicating disc from plywood and drill a hole in the centre. This should be slightly larger in diameter than the plastic pipe to allow it to slide up and down easily. Drop it over the top of the pole.

6 Cut out the piece of timber for the top arm and drill a hole for the top of the dowel rod pole. Screw a hook in to each end of this arm. Glue the arm on to the dowel rod.

7 Make a scale by painting numbers on to a length of timber. You could also use plastic tape to mark off the sections. I suggest you place the numbers at different distances and make it very hard to reach 4 and 5 on the scale. Drill a hole at the top so that it can be hung on one of the hooks in the top arm.

8 Shape up the mallet head from a block of soft wood. Drill a hole for the dowel rod handle and glue a rubber pad on to each of the two striking surfaces.

Cut the handle to length and drill a hole through the end for a piece of cord. Tie a loop of cord through the hole so that the mallet can be hung up on the other hook on the top arm.

Glue the handle *very* securely into the mallet head.

9 Glasspaper the toy all over and use bright non-toxic exterior paints (see page 95) and plastic tape to make the strength-tester worthy of any fairground or fête.

Cutting list

Lateral base cross bar	1 off	610 × 64 × 44mm (24 × 2½ × 1¾in)	Timber
Fore and aft base cross member	1 off	610 × 64 × 44mm (24 × 2½ × 1¾in)	Timber
	1 off	178 × 64 × 44mm (7 × 2½ × 1¾in)	Timber
	1 off	140 × 64 × 44mm (5½ × 2½ × 1¾in)	Timber
Vertical pole	1 off	1475mm (58in) × 20mm (¾in) diam dowelling	
Top arm	1 off	305 × 44 × 44mm (12 × 1¾ × 1¾in)	Timber
Height indicating disc	1 off	140 × 140 × 9mm (5½ × 5½ × ⅜in)	Plywood
Fork end	1 off	292 × 102 × 6mm (11½ × 4 × ¼in)	Plywood
Target area	1 off	140 × 140 × 6mm (5½ × 5½ × ¼in)	Plywood
Pivot beam	1 off	457 × 35 × 25mm (18 × 1½ × 1in)	Timber
	2 off	165 × 35 × 25mm (6½ × 1½ × 1in)	Timber
Scale	1 off	635 × 44 × 12mm (25 × 1¾ × ½in)	Timber
Mallet	1 off	127 × 95 × 70mm (5 × 3¾ × 2¾in)	Timber
	1 off	508mm (20in) × 22mm (⅞in) diam dowelling	

Ancillaries

	2 off	20mm (¾in) screwed eyes
	2 off	20mm (¾in) screwed hooks
	1 off	1475mm (58in) × 22mm (⅞in) ¹diam plastic water waste pipe
	1 off	25mm (1in) steel hinge
	1 off	305mm (12in) length 3mm (⅛in) square 'catapult' elastic and lashing thread

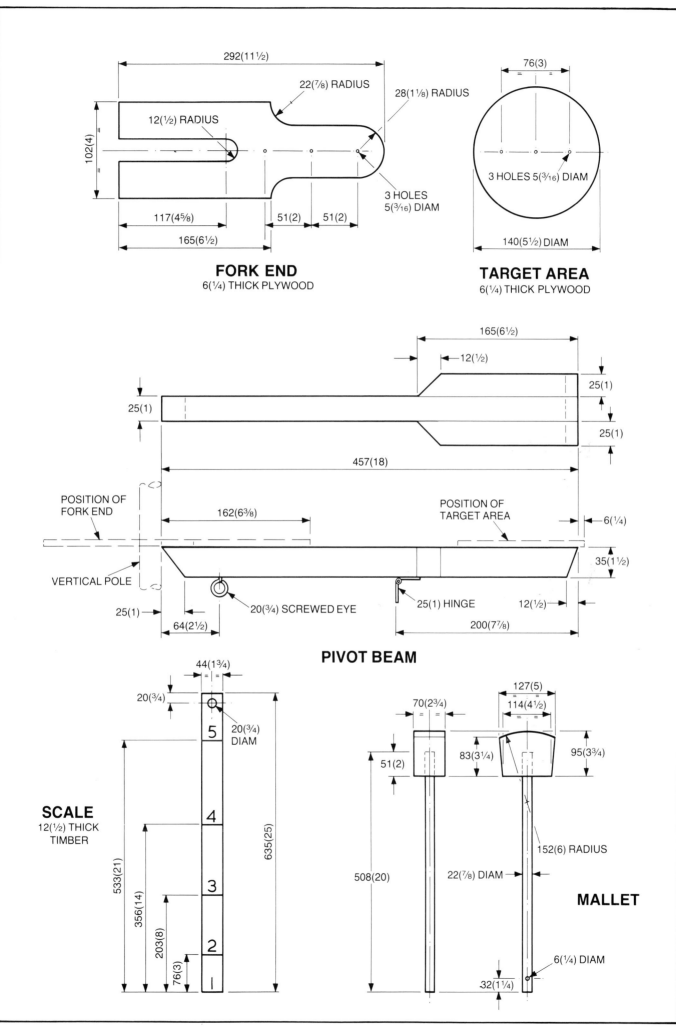

FORK END
6(¼) THICK PLYWOOD

TARGET AREA
6(¼) THICK PLYWOOD

292(11½)

22(⅞) RADIUS

28(1⅛) RADIUS

12(½) RADIUS

102(4)

3 HOLES
5(³⁄₁₆) DIAM

117(4⅝)

51(2)

51(2)

165(6½)

76(3)

3 HOLES 5(³⁄₁₆) DIAM

140(5½) DIAM

165(6½)

12(½)

25(1)

25(1)

25(1)

457(18)

POSITION OF
FORK END

162(6⅜)

POSITION OF
TARGET AREA

6(¼)

VERTICAL POLE

35(1½)

25(1)

20(¾) SCREWED EYE

25(1) HINGE

12(½)

64(2½)

200(7⅞)

PIVOT BEAM

44(1¾)

20(¾)

20(¾)
DIAM

5

4

3

2

1

635(25)

533(21)

356(14)

203(8)

76(3)

SCALE
12(½) THICK
TIMBER

127(5)

114(4½)

70(2¾)

51(2)

83(3¼)

95(3¾)

152(6) RADIUS

508(20)

22(⅞) DIAM

MALLET

6(¼) DIAM

32(1¼)

11

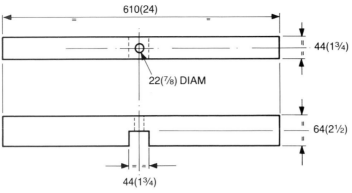

610(24)

44(1¾)

22(⅞) DIAM

64(2½)

44(1¾)

LATERAL BASE CROSS BAR

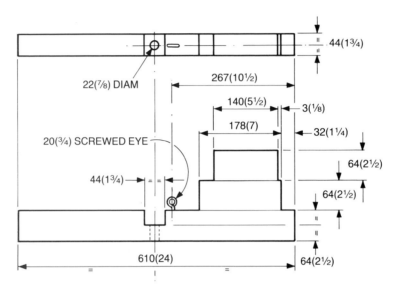

44(1¾)

22(⅞) DIAM

267(10½)

140(5½)

3(⅛)

178(7)

32(1¼)

20(¾) SCREWED EYE

64(2½)

44(1¾)

64(2½)

610(24)

64(2½)

FORE & AFT BASE CROSS MEMBER

VERTICAL POLE MAKE FROM 22(⅞) OUTSIDE DIAM × 1475(58) LONG PLASTIC WATER
PIPE WITH A 20(¾) DIAM WOODEN DOWEL FITTED FULL LENGTH
DOWN ITS BORE

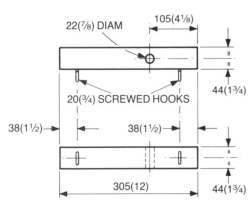

22(⅞) DIAM

105(4⅛)

44(1¾)

20(¾) SCREWED HOOKS

38(1½)

38(1½)

305(12)

44(1¾)

TOP ARM

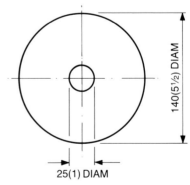

140(5½) DIAM

25(1) DIAM

HEIGHT INDICATING DISC
9(⅜) THICK PLYWOOD

SWING

This garden plaything must be the most popular that has ever been devised. I have tried to avoid one or two problems that do occur when designing and making a free-standing swing. The bases are very long and the swing is braced at the sides so you don't need to secure it into the ground. If you fit a plywood base it will prevent the mud puddle which is so often found beneath swings, and the dangerous concrete that usually fills the hole after the first season's use.

Today many gardens are fairly small and there are more paved patio areas than ever before. This swing is ideal for such locations, the only requirement being a flat piece of ground to set it up. Just in case you have a budding Tarzan in the family I have allowed for extra guy ropes to be threaded through the top bars allowing the swing to be guy roped – just like a tent.

The wooden swing seat can be dangerous and it is therefore a good idea to pad the front and sides with rubber to avoid any accidents. This is not a difficult project so don't be daunted by the size of some of the pieces of wood.

I Start by marking out all the uprights for the side frames – the two vertical legs and the four legs for the bracing frame assembly. Mark each category out together to ensure accuracy. Be particularly careful to mark out the trenches on the vertical legs carefully. These are for the cross members of the bracing frames to fit into. Once you are sure your marking out is accurate, cut out

all the uprights, cut out all the halving joints (see page 90) and the angles on the ends of the bracing frame assembly legs. Drill holes in the vertical legs for the coach bolts.

2 Now mark and cut out the other pieces of timber needed for the side frames: the facing plate mounting blocks which fit on the top of the vertical legs,

the cross members for the vertical leg bracing frame assembly, which needs three halving joints, and the corner blocks for the bracing frame.

3 Lay out all the pieces for the side frames on a large flat surface and check everything fits together properly. Then glue and screw the side frames together using waterproof glue and zinc-plated screws that won't rust.

4 Now mark and cut out all the cross members for the base. Four of these are exactly the same length and have halving joints cut on the ends, so it is a good idea to mark these out together. The central cross member, however, is longer and in addition to needing two trenches for the longitudinal base members to fit into, it also needs holes drilled for the coach bolts that will fix the lateral bracing ties in place.

When the cross members are finished, cut the two longitudinal base members to length, and mark and cut out the three trenches for the side frame uprights to fit into. (I also cut angles (see page 90) on the ends of these base members for no other reason than that I think it looks better.)

5 Now glue and screw the longitudinal and cross members together to form a good solid base. With the help of an assistant, glue and screw each side frame into place. Cut to length the two lateral bracing ties, cut the angles needed on the bottom of each and drill holes for the coach bolts. Fix the ties on to the vertical legs and central base cross member with coach bolts. Saw off any protruding bolt ends (see page 94), file the ends smooth and cover them with plastic insulation tape for both safety reasons and weather protection.

6 Cut out the upper cross member that will hold the ropes for the swing. This piece of timber projects out over the vertical legs and can be drilled with holes for guy ropes, should they be required. Drill the holes for the swing ropes. Glue and screw the upper cross member into place on top of the vertical legs and between the facing plate mounting blocks. These blocks give extra rigidity since the upper cross member will take a lot of strain when the swing is in use, as do the two upper member facing plates, which you should cut out and glue and screw in position on each side of the upper cross member.

7 Finally you are ready to hang the seat. Cut it out and drill the holes for the ropes. Round off the edges with a spokeshave and glasspaper it carefully so that it is really smooth. Ideally you should fit rubber round the edges to avoid a child being hurt if hit by it.

My method of roping the seat was simply to thread a length of rope through the two holes on each side of the seat, take the two ends up through the predrilled hole in the cross member and knot them together with massive knots that couldn't possibly be pulled back through the hole.

8 Finish off the swing by sandpapering off any sharp edges and see page 95 for advice on wood preservatives and exterior paints.

Cutting list

Base – cross members	4 off	730 × 70 × 44mm (28¾ × 2¾ × 1¾in)	Timber
	1 off	1530 × 70 × 44mm (60¼ × 2¾ × 1¾in)	Timber
Base – longitudinal	2 off	1505 × 70 × 44mm (59¼ × 2¾ × 1¾in)	Timber
Bracing frame	2 off	788 × 70 × 44mm (31 × 2¾ × 1¾in)	Timber
	1 off	610 × 70 × 40mm (24 × 2¾ × 1¾in)	Timber
Flooring	1 off	1465 × 641 × 3mm (57¾ × 25¼ × ⅛in)	Plywood
Leg	2 off	1848 × 70 × 44mm (72¾ × 2¾ × 1¾in)	Timber
Bracing	4 off	1403 × 51 × 22mm (55¼ × 2 × ⅞in)	Timber
Upper cross member	1 off	940 × 70 × 44mm (37 × 2¾ × 1¾in)	Timber
Facing plates	2 off	775 × 121 × 22mm (30½ × 4¾ × ⅞in)	Timber
Mounting blocks	4 off	286 × 44 × 38mm (11¼ × 1¾ × 1½in)	Timber
Seat	1 off	508 × 248 × 22mm (20 × 9¾ × ⅞in)	Timber
Ancillaries			
	4 off	127mm (5in) long × 9mm (⅜in) coach bolt	
	Make from	7.25 mm (24ft) stout nylon cord	

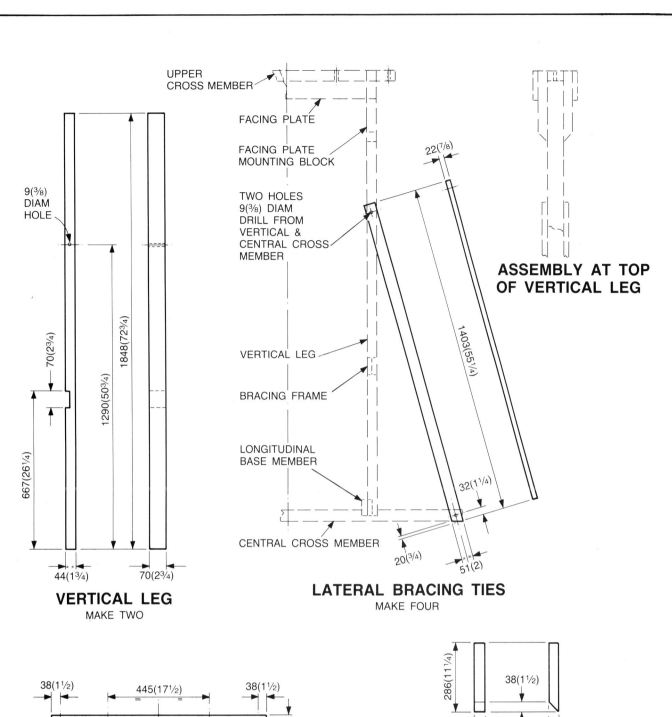

9(3/8)
DIAM
HOLE

70(2³/₄)

1848(72³/₄)

1290(50³/₄)

667(26¹/₄)

44(1³/₄)   70(2³/₄)

VERTICAL LEG
MAKE TWO

UPPER
CROSS MEMBER

FACING PLATE

FACING PLATE
MOUNTING BLOCK

TWO HOLES
9(3/8) DIAM
DRILL FROM
VERTICAL &
CENTRAL CROSS
MEMBER

VERTICAL LEG

BRACING FRAME

LONGITUDINAL
BASE MEMBER

CENTRAL CROSS MEMBER

22(⁷/₈)

1403(55¹/₄)

32(1¹/₄)

20(³/₄)

51(2)

ASSEMBLY AT TOP
OF VERTICAL LEG

LATERAL BRACING TIES
MAKE FOUR

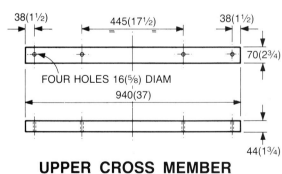

38(1¹/₂)   445(17¹/₂)   38(1¹/₂)

70(2³/₄)

FOUR HOLES 16(⁵/₈) DIAM

940(37)

44(1³/₄)

UPPER CROSS MEMBER

UPPER MEMBER FACING PLATES
775 x 121 x 22(30¹/₂ x 4³/₄ x ⁷/₈)
MAKE TWO

286(11¹/₄)

38(1¹/₂)

44(1³/₄)   38(1¹/₂)

FACING PLATE
MOUNTING BLOCKS
MAKE FOUR

FOUR HOLES 12(¹/₂) DIAM

191(7¹/₂)

248(9³/₄)

445(17¹/₂)

508(20)

SEAT
22(⁷/₈) THICK

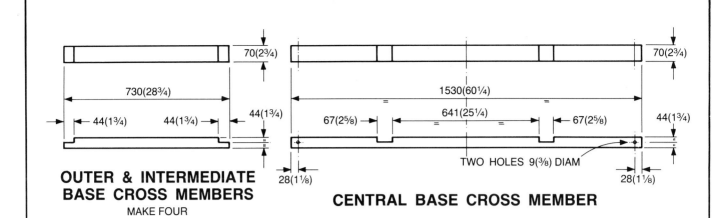

OUTER & INTERMEDIATE BASE CROSS MEMBERS
MAKE FOUR

70(2¾)
730(28¾)
44(1¾)
44(1¾)
44(1¾)

CENTRAL BASE CROSS MEMBER

70(2¾)
1530(60¼)
641(25¼)
67(2⅝)
67(2⅝)
44(1¾)
TWO HOLES 9(⅜) DIAM
28(1⅛)
28(1⅛)

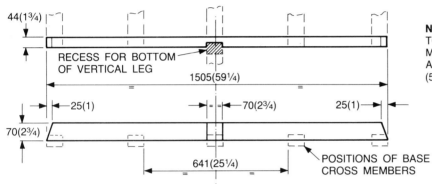

44(1¾)
RECESS FOR BOTTOM OF VERTICAL LEG
1505(59¼)
25(1)
70(2¾)
25(1)
70(2¾)
641(25¼)
POSITIONS OF BASE CROSS MEMBERS

LONGITUDINAL BASE MEMBERS
MAKE TWO

NOTE:
TOP SURFACE OF BASE CROSS MEMBERS TO BE SKINNED WITH A PIECE OF 1465 x 641 x 3 (57¾ × 25¼ × ⅛) THICK PLYWOOD

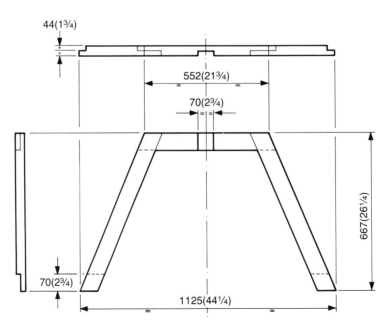

44(1¾)
552(21¾)
70(2¾)
667(26¼)
70(2¾)
1125(44¼)

VERTICAL LEG BRACING FRAME ASSEMBLY
MAKE TWO FROM 70(2¾) x 44(1¾) TIMBER

SLIDE

Slides and helter-skelters hold a particular fascination for active youngsters. The adrenalin they gain from zooming down the slide seems to give them the energy to race from the bottom back up to the top of the steps for another go.

I made this toy from Nordic redwood and 'far eastern' plywood, but, if you can afford it, Finnish plywood is better. It is more expensive but tends to splinter less.

The climbing frame

1 Start by preparing the four uprights – or 'stringers' – for the two ladders that form the frame. The stringers have to have slots, or 'trenches', cut in them to take the rungs and these must be carefully marked out. If you mark out all four together you will achieve greater accuracy and save a great deal of time.

Once the marking out is done, fit two uprights in the vice at a time and, using a tenon saw (see page 91) cut down the

sides for each trench and then use a large firmer chisel (see page 91) to remove the waste wood at the bottom. As you are chiselling across the grain of the wood, the waste will come out very easily.

2 When all the trenches have been cut, you can start work on the rungs. There are a total of eight, four for each ladder. Clamp all eight together with the sides (i.e. narrowest edges) facing you. Mark out a rebate on each end of each rung

(see page 90). These rebates will make the ladders very stable when assembled. Un-clamp the rungs and cut out the rebates with a tenon saw. Check that each fits snugly in the trenches on the stringers as you go.

3   Before assembling the ladders you need to do some more work on the stringers. The bottoms of each stringer need to be cut off at an angle so that when the frame is opened out the feet stand firmly on the ground (see 'side view' of climbing frame' on page 19). Using a sliding bevel gauge (see page 90), mark out the angles and cut away the waste with a tenon saw. Double-check, before you cut, that you have marked the angle correctly on the right side of the stringers.

An angle also has to be cut at the top of the stringers for the front ladder (i.e. the one used for climbing up to the slide). This is so that, when the frame is opened, the tops of the ladders butt together.

Once all the angles have been cut, chamfer off around the bottom of each stringer (see page 91 and 94) using a block plane or chisel. This simple precaution will prevent the ends splintering if the slide is dragged along the ground.

Drill holes in the rear stringers to take the hand rail, and in all the stringers for the hinges that will hold the two ladders together.

4   Now you are ready to assemble the ladders. Lay the stringers on the bench in pairs and glue and screw the rungs in place. Use zinc-plated screws that won't rust and stain your handiwork. Both glue *and* screws are essential for this since the frame has to withstand several children climbing up and sliding off at one time.

5   Cut out the two hand rails and, in each, drill a hole at the top for the hand rope and two holes at the bottom for the coach bolts. Coach bolt the hand rail on to the inside of the rear stringers.

6   Fit the two ladders together using black 'japanned' or zinc hinges. Ordinary steel hinges will rust. Thread lengths of strong rope through the holes in the top of the hand rails down to the second rung of the front ladder. Knot them firmly in place. Make sure you use good rope and very good knots as young children will cling fast to these ropes as they climb up.

7   Assemble the platform for the top of the frame which is simply two slats screwed to cross-pieces of timber. Note that the slats should be chamfered so that there are no sharp edges to cut children as they sit down ready for their slide. This platform fits snugly in place on top of the opened-out frame. Use two long screws to hold it firmly to the frame.

The slide

If you watch children at play on a slide you discover that they not only slide down, but also enjoy turning round at the bottom and trying to run back up the slide. Some children will also run down slides and others will ride BMX bikes up them! Therefore this slide is built like a battleship.

I   Cut the slide side members to length. Round off the bottom ends using a spokeshave. Mark out the angles needed at the top ends and cut away the waste wood with a tenon saw.

Clamp both members together and mark the places where the cross members are to go.

2   Cut all six cross members to length. Clamp them together, with the narrowest edges facing you, and mark out the positions for the rebates on the ends. Using a tenon saw, cut away the waste pieces.

Lay the side members out on a large flat surface (i.e. the floor!) and fit all the cross members in position. Glue and screw each one in place using long screws with a minimum gauge of No. 8. This is important as the slide frame needs to be very strong.

3   Turn the frame over and measure very carefully the piece of plywood you'll need for the base. If you marked all your cross members out accurately and fitted them carefully you should find the width is constant right down the length of the slide. If it isn't you'll have to measure out your plywood even more carefully (better luck next time!).

Cut out the plywood and fix it to the cross members with zinc-plated screws. These must be countersunk (see page 93) so that the screw-heads don't scratch the slide-users.

Assembling and finishing

I   To assemble the slide, open out the climbing frame fully. Fit the platform on top and then fit the slide on to the frame. The top cross member of the slide fits snugly over the top rung of the rear ladder and you should end up with a firm and stable structure with no 'movement'.

2   Plywood can give some very nasty splinters so make sure you carry out the following before you let your children use the slide:
i   glasspaper the entire structure, but particularly the plywood sliding area.
ii   seal the plywood with three coats of polyurethane varnish, glasspapering thoroughly between each coat. This will, of course, also increase the slide's slipperiness. However, it also means you should not leave it out in the rain unless you are prepared to sand it off and re-varnish it every year (see page 95).

Cutting list

Rung	8 off	700 × 70 × 44mm (27½ × 2¾ × 1¾in)	Timber
Forward stringer	2 off	1385 × 70 × 44mm (54½ × 2¾ × 1¾in)	Timber
Rear stringer	2 off	1372 × 70 × 44mm (54 × 2¾ × 1¾in)	Timber
Platform	2 off	610 × 95 × 22mm (24 × 3¾ × ⅞in)	Timber
	2 off	318 × 70 × 44mm (12½ × 2¾ × 1¾in)	Timber
Hand rail	2 off	622 × 44 × 44mm (24½ × 1¾ × 1¾in)	Timber
Slide cross members	6 off	470 × 70 × 44mm (18½ × 2¾ × 1¾in)	Timber
Slide side members	2 off	2100 × 95 × 35mm (82¾ × 3¾ × 1⅜in)	Timber
Slide surface	I off	2032 × 400 × 9mm (80 × 15¾ × ⅜in)	Plywood

Ancillaries

	2 off	Hinges
	4 off	102mm (4in) × 6mm (¼in) coach bolts, washers and wing nuts
	2 off	1525mm (60in) lengths of strong nylon cord

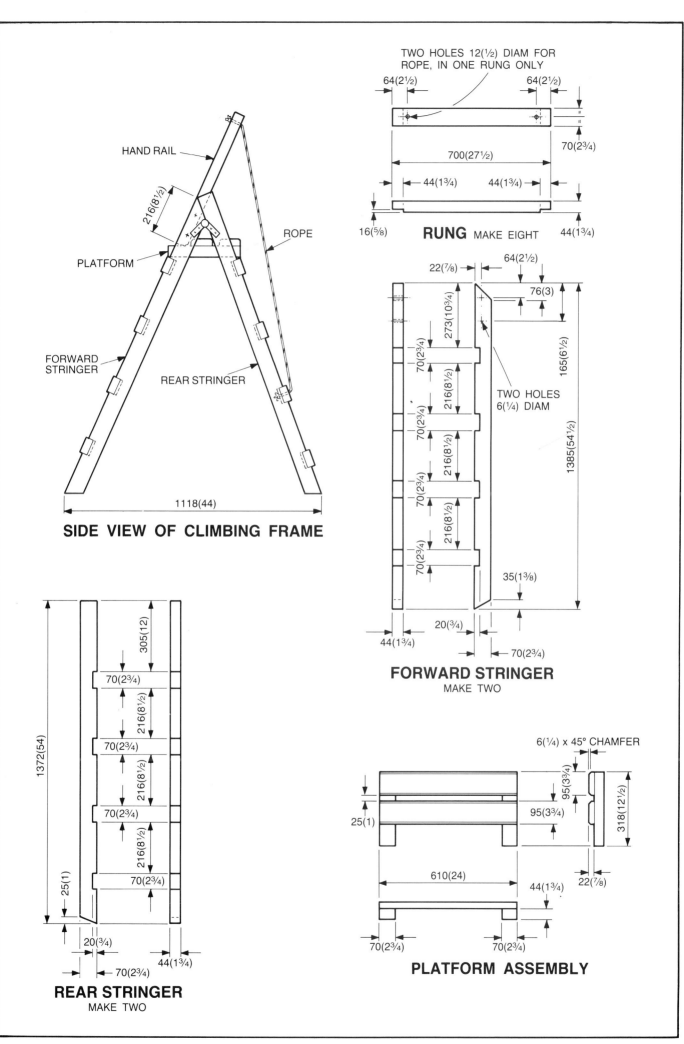

SIDE VIEW OF CLIMBING FRAME

TWO HOLES 12(½) DIAM FOR ROPE, IN ONE RUNG ONLY

64(2½) 64(2½)

700(27½)

44(1¾) 44(1¾)

70(2¾)

16(⅝) 44(1¾)

RUNG MAKE EIGHT

22(⅞) 64(2½)

76(3)

273(10¾)

70(2¾)

165(6½)

216(8½)

70(2¾)

TWO HOLES 6(¼) DIAM

216(8½)

1385(54½)

70(2¾)

216(8½)

70(2¾)

35(1⅜)

20(¾)

44(1¾) 70(2¾)

FORWARD STRINGER
MAKE TWO

305(12)

70(2¾)

216(8½)

1372(54)

70(2¾)

216(8½)

70(2¾)

216(8½)

70(2¾)

25(1)

20(¾) 44(1¾)

70(2¾)

REAR STRINGER
MAKE TWO

6(¼) x 45° CHAMFER

95(3¾)

95(3¾)

318(12½)

25(1)

610(24)

44(1¾)

22(⅞)

70(2¾) 70(2¾)

PLATFORM ASSEMBLY

HAND RAIL

216(8½)

PLATFORM

ROPE

FORWARD STRINGER

REAR STRINGER

1118(44)

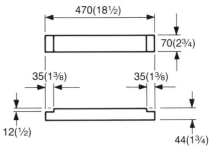

SLIDE CROSS MEMBERS
MAKE SIX

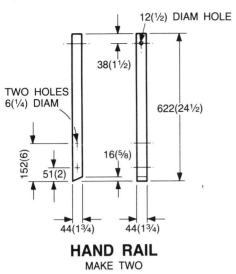

12(½) DIAM HOLE

38(1½)

622(24½)

TWO HOLES
6(¼) DIAM

152(6)

51(2)

16(⅝)

44(1¾)   44(1¾)

HAND RAIL
MAKE TWO

470(18½)

70(2¾)

35(1⅜)   35(1⅜)

12(½)

44(1¾)

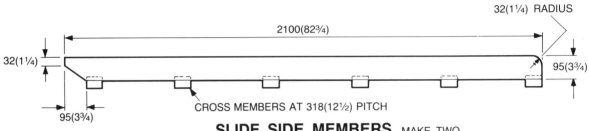

32(1¼) RADIUS

2100(82¾)

32(1¼)

95(3¾)

95(3¾)

CROSS MEMBERS AT 318(12½) PITCH

SLIDE SIDE MEMBERS MAKE TWO
35(1⅜) THICK TIMBER

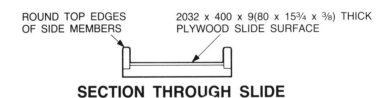

ROUND TOP EDGES
OF SIDE MEMBERS

2032 x 400 x 9(80 x 15¾ x ⅜) THICK
PLYWOOD SLIDE SURFACE

SECTION THROUGH SLIDE

SEE-SAW

An ever popular toy with all ages, children just love being rocketed up into the air on a see-saw and equally relish the thump as they come back to earth. This design allows for rapid assembly and dismantling – the board can stand upright in your shed or garage and the stand can hang on the wall. Children of different weights can easily find the correct balance position as I have allowed a long seating area and good handles.

I used Nordic redwood timber and ramin dowel rods. It is probably best to buy the dowel rod necessary before getting to work in case you can't get the exact diameter specified, in which case you will need to alter the size of the holes you drill accordingly. If you can't find thick enough dowelling, then two strong broom handles will do.

1   Start by making the stand, which consists of two identical side frames held together with dowel rods. It's a good idea to mark both frames out at the same time. The joints used are halving joints (see page 90) which are a little more tricky to cut than usual as they are at an angle. I have always found that the success of any woodworking project is the marking out and for this job of marking out the angled halving joints you really do need a marking gauge *and* a sliding bevel gauge (see page 90). Following the plans, mark out everything in pencil and once the bevel gauge is set, mark all the angles with it. On no account alter the bevel gauge!

Now the old adage of measuring twice and cutting once is particularly applicable here. Once marked out in pencil, go over the whole job again to make sure that you are going to cut off the right pieces. Using a pencil, 'scribble out' the areas you will cut off to be doubly sure you have got it right. 'Assemble' the frame dry and think it through – will it work? Once you are sure, go over all the pencil lines with a marking knife (see page 90), again using your sliding bevel gauge to help you.

2   Cut out all the joints with a tenon saw and assemble them dry again to check that all fits well. It's at this stage you will be glad you marked out accurately! Now glue each frame together and, once the glue is dry, add a couple of screws to each joint – see-saws get worked terribly hard so it's worth the 'belt and braces' approach here.

3   Now for the dowel rods that hold the frames together. Mark the position of the dowel rods carefully and drill the holes using a large flat bit. If you have a drill stand the job is simple, but if not, then get an assistant to help you line up the electric drill at 90° in both planes (see page 93). This drilling process is a vital one and if the holes are not bored accurately then the two frames will not line up and the work will be spoilt.

Once the holes have been bored, glue all the dowel rods into one framework first. The protruding ends will then need to be chamfered off (see page 91) to make it easier to fit them into the second frame. Apply glue to the ends and

then, using a large hammer and a block of waste wood (to prevent damage to the frame), tap the second frame onto the protruding dowel rods. The most difficult bit is getting started. Once all the dowel rods are into the holes you have to work quickly using the hammer and block of wood to drive the framework onto the rods. When the dowel rods are flush with the outside face of the frame the job is done. After the glue has dried, plane off any glue residue or rough wood.

4   Once the stand is completed you can start work on the seat. It's important to try to find a piece of wood that is fairly knot-free for the main plank otherwise it won't be strong enough.

The plank gets its strength from the two pieces of wood or 'stiffeners' that you must fit on the top. Use a coping saw or jigsaw (see page 91) to cut the shaping out and then drill the holes to take the dowel rod handles. You will find a spokeshave (see page 91) invaluable to finish off the middle section once all the 'roughing out' has been done. Now glue and screw these two stiffeners on to the main plank from underneath. You will find it helpful to fit the dowel rod handles in position before fixing the stiffeners on to the plank.

5   Using a spokeshave, remove all the sharp edges from the seat areas. Make sure they are really smooth and round off the corners.

6   All see-saws need 'bump blocks' fitted beneath the seats. These blocks prevent children's feet getting trapped under the plank so they are essential. Fix them with at least three 65–75mm (2½–3in) No. 8 gauge screws each.

7   The plank is fixed to the stand by two sections of timber (pivot blocks) that you must screw onto the underside of the main plank. Initially these should be positioned fairly tight up against the 'pivot' dowel rod at the top of the stand as they will obviously loosen up with use. By making the blocks fairly deep (see plans) you will avoid any possibility of the main plank slipping off the stand.

8   Finish off the see-saw with a good sandpapering, and see page 95 for advice on wood preservatives and exterior paints.

Cutting list

Main plank	1 off	2440 × 197 × 22mm (96 × 7¾ × ⅞in)	Timber
Stiffeners	2 off	1510 × 95 × 22mm (59½ × 3¾ × ⅞in)	Timber
Bump blocks	2 off	178 × 95 × 44mm (7 × 3¾ × 1¾in)	Timber
Pivot blocks	2 off	191 × 70 × 44mm (7½ × 2¾ × 1¾in)	Timber
Handles	2 off	394mm (15½in) × 22mm (⅞in) diam dowelling	
Stand frames	2 off	915 × 70 × 44mm (36 × 2¾ × 1¾in)	Timber
	4 off	690 × 70 × 44mm (27⅛ × 2¾ × 1¾in)	Timber
	7 off	305mm (12in) × 22mm (⅞in) diam dowelling	

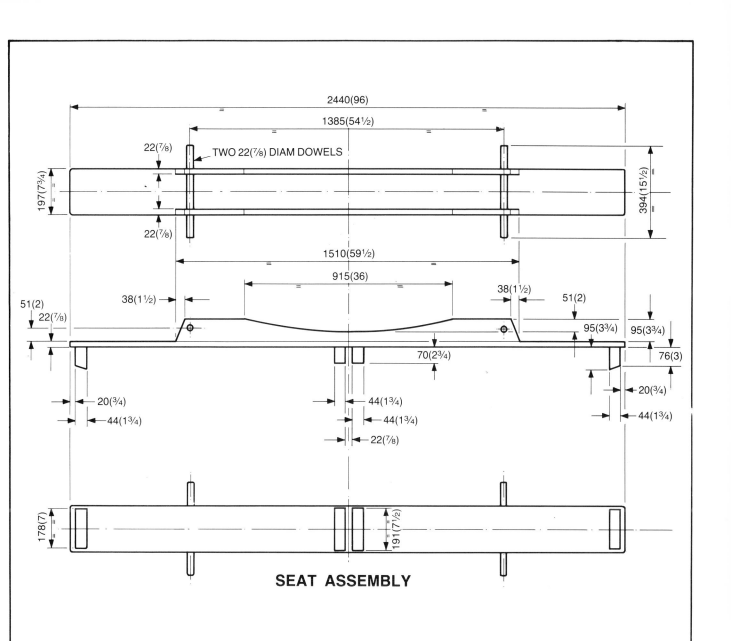

SEAT ASSEMBLY

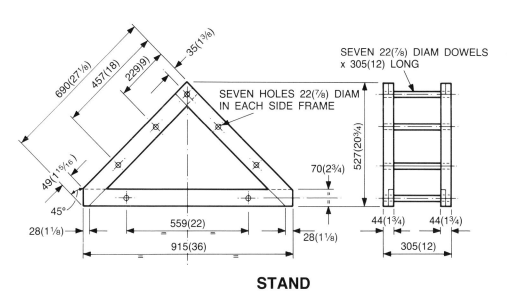

STAND

FRAME CONSTRUCTED IN 70 × 44(2¾ × 1¾) TIMBER

MARKET STALL

After a period of building rather soul-less shopping centres, many of our towns have gone back to serving their customers in the traditional way, and squares and streets are once again thronged with market traders. This cheerful market stall will help children create the fun of 'keeping shop'. The job is rather like making a deck chair – lots of bits and pieces that fold up, with lengths of cord to act as stays when the legs and frame are fully extended.

This is a very easy project as the woodworking is straightforward and I used deck chair canvas and carpet tape for the roof – simple!

Making the frames

1   If you study the plans you will see that the stall consists basically of two rectangular wooden frames and a front leg section. It is simplest to prepare all the wooden battens you will need first.

Cut all the timber to length and assemble the various pieces on your workshop bench, garage floor or large kitchen table, and work out how things go together!

2   Make the back frame (i.e. the frame nearest the stall holder) first. Take the two vertical battens and drill holes in them at the top for the cord stays and at the bottom for the bolts that hold the two frames together.

Now take the two cross members (i.e. the horizontal battens that hold the vertical pieces together at the top and in the middle). Cut rebates (really half a halving joint – see page 90) on the ends of both cross members. This will mean that when glued and screwed onto the verticals the joints will have extra rigidity. After you have assembled the complete frame in this way, check that it is square before the glue dries and adjust as necessary.

3   The second, or front, frame is made in a similar way to the first, but in addition to drilling holes at the top and bottom of the verticals, you also need to drill them in the centre and also just up from the bottom, as shown on the plans, to take the bolts and stays that will hold on the leg section. Only one cross member, rebated, glued and screwed to the top of the verticals, is needed.

If all this is beginning to sound like the woodworker's guide to 'cat's cradle', don't worry! It's really not as difficult as it sounds.

4   Now make the leg section. Cut an angle on the top of the verticals so that, when fully extended, they provide a flat support for the counter top (see page 27). Drill the holes at the top for the bolts that will fix the leg section to the front frame. Rebate the cross member, drill the holes for the stays, and glue and screw it across the bottom of the verticals.

Assembling the frames

Now you are ready to fix these three frames together. For this sort of job I would normally use coach bolts, but they are quite expensive and don't always come to the length you require. I always find myself having to buy a bolt that is too long and then hacksaw off the end. So to avoid this waste I elected to use 'studding'. This is a length of mild (i.e. soft) steel bar that has a thread running along its length. It comes in various different diameters, and nuts and washers are available that match the thread. Simply buy a length of studding and, using a small hacksaw, cut off the lengths you require. A useful tip is to thread the nuts you will need on to the bar before you cut it up since the sawing often creates 'burrs' that might make it tricky to thread them on afterwards. If any burrs cause you problems, use a smooth cut file to remove them.

1   Cut to length four pieces of studding or coach bolts (see page 94) and use them to fix the front and back frames together at the bottom and to attach the leg section to the front frame at counter height. Always fit washers beneath the nuts and be sure you have filed off any sharp edges on the studding (or bolts).

2   Cut lengths of cord and thread them in place at the top of the two main frames and also between the leg section and front frame at the bottom to act as stays when the shop is 'open'.

3   Mark and cut out the counter and, if you wish, cover it with self-adhesive plastic. The counter just sits on the middle batten and top of the leg section and should fit snugly in position.

4   To make the roof canopy and front apron use either cotton or nylon deck chair canvas. The nylon variety stays cleaner and has the added advantage that it can be joined together with carpet tape easily. (My first attempts with a sewing machine on cotton canvas are best forgotten!)

Join pieces together until you have the right width and trim with brightly coloured carpet tape to prevent it fraying. I cut a scalloped edge for extra decoration.

5 Once you have made the canopy and apron, extend the shop framework to its full width and tack the canvas in place using brass-headed pins. (Someone to hold the shop steady while you do this is a boon.)

When you want to put the shop away, simply remove the counter top and fold up the framework. For those times when it rains on market day you should follow the advice on page 95 regarding wood preservatives and paints.

Cutting list

Verticals	4 off	1515 × 44 × 22mm (59⅝ × 1¾ × ⅞in)	Timber
Leg	2 off	813 × 44 × 22mm (32 × 1¾ × ⅞in)	Timber
Cross members	2 off	819 × 44 × 22mm (32¼ × 1¾ × ⅞in)	Timber
	1 off	775 × 44 × 22mm (30½ × 1¾ × ⅞in)	Timber
	1 off '	730 × 44 × 22mm (28¾ × 1¾ × ⅞in)	Timber
Counter	1 off	775 × 387 × 9mm (30½ × 15¼ × ⅜in)	Plywood

Ancillaries

	4 off	64mm (2½in) × 6mm (¼in) coach bolts, washers and wing nuts
	Make from	1830mm (72in) strong cord
	1 off	914mm (36in) × 700mm (27½in) deckchair canvas
	1 off	775mm (30½in) × 355mm (14in) deckchair canvas

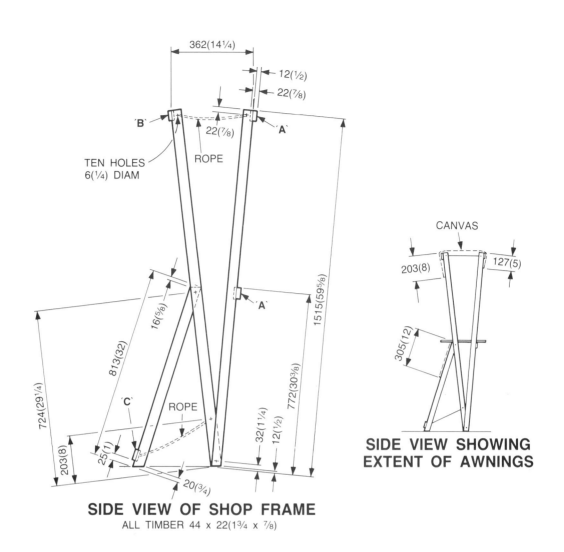

362(14¼)
12(½)
22(⅞)
22(⅞)
'B'
'A'
ROPE
TEN HOLES
6(¼) DIAM
16(⅝)
'A'
813(32)
1515(59⅝)
724(29¼)
'C'
ROPE
203(8)
25(1)
772(30⅜)
32(1¼)
12(½)
20(¾)

SIDE VIEW OF SHOP FRAME
ALL TIMBER 44 x 22(1¾ x ⅞)

CANVAS
203(8)
127(5)
305(12)

**SIDE VIEW SHOWING
EXTENT OF AWNINGS**

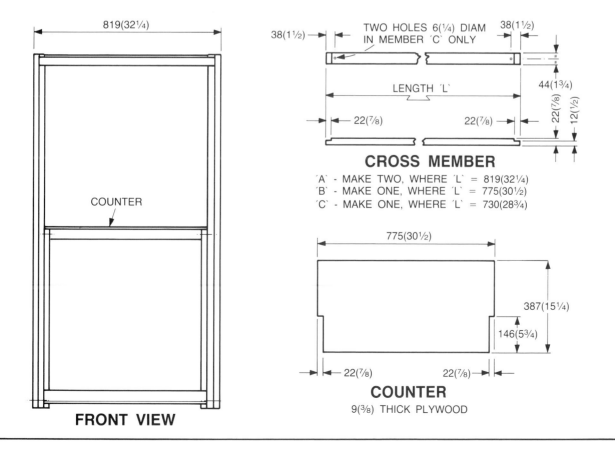

819(32¼)

COUNTER

FRONT VIEW

38(1½)
TWO HOLES 6(¼) DIAM
IN MEMBER 'C' ONLY
38(1½)
LENGTH 'L'
44(1¾)
22(⅞)
22(⅞)
22(⅞)
12(½)

CROSS MEMBER

'A' - MAKE TWO, WHERE 'L' = 819(32¼)
'B' - MAKE ONE, WHERE 'L' = 775(30½)
'C' - MAKE ONE, WHERE 'L' = 730(28¾)

775(30½)
387(15¼)
146(5¾)
22(⅞)
22(⅞)

COUNTER
9(⅜) THICK PLYWOOD

VIKING LONGBOAT

If you ever stop to watch and listen to children playing you will be surprised to discover just how fertile their imaginations are. A large cardboard box becomes a Norman castle, the humble tricycle a chariot pulled by four magnificent horses, and a blanket over a clothes horse one of the most dangerous forests of South America.

This Viking longboat enters into this spirit of imagination providing the chance for adventure and seamanship from a bygone age, without the need for Lloyd's to underwrite the project!

The construction only involves plywood, some large dowel rods, deck chair canvas and several reels of coloured tape for shield decoration. I have tried to be economical, and therefore most of the boat can be made from one 8′ × 4′ sheet of plywood. However, you'll need to cut the dragon head and some of the shields from an extra sheet. Because of the length and nature of the shaping it is essential to have a jigsaw to cut out the boat sides. You can't use a bow or coping saw.

The hull

1   Make a start by selecting your sheet of plywood. The best type to choose is Finnish birch-faced plywood as this is top-quality 'genuine' plywood. However, just to see if my design worked with the far more common Far Eastern plywood, I made my boat from that and it was fine. The only problem that may arise is that when the middle is bowed to form the *beam* (i.e. the width of the boat), one of the plywood sides may crack, so you should bend the plywood very carefully at the initial stages.

2   Following the plans, mark out the two sides (see page 30). With a jigsaw (and possibly someone to help hold the end of the plywood sheet), cut the sides out. You'll end up with a large waste piece which you can use for shields.

Some plywoods give very nasty splinters, and the next thing you'll need to do is glasspaper smooth the sawn edges. If you get a long 'spilch' that has broken away from the side, but is still attached, glue it back into place and use a length of

masking tape to hold it there while the glue dries. Genuine plywood does not produce as many spilch problems as the Far Eastern plywoods. Do bear in mind that children will be climbing over the side of the boat and unless you are careful to make the plywood edges safe at this stage, nasty scratches will occur.

3   Tape the two sides together and drill the holes at either end to take the lacing of cord that will hold them together. When you are drilling these holes, place a piece of waste wood underneath. Otherwise when the bit comes through you will have a 'gribbly' hole with spilches and splinters worthy of a porcupine!

4   Mark and cut out the piece of timber for the head post at the prow (front) of the ship. This has to have holes drilled through it corresponding to those in the plywood sides – be sure to drill them at 90° in both planes (see page 93) and the right distance apart. Shape the two curves smoothly with a spokeshave and cut out the slot for the head with a tenon and a coping saw.

5 The dragon's head for the prow gives plenty of scope for creative flair. Make a template (see page 90), following the plans, and use it to mark out the shape on to plywood. Cut it out using a jigsaw and glasspaper the edges. Cut teeth and eyes from offcuts of timber and glue them in position.

I advise just pushing the head into position in the head post, rather than glueing it there, so that you can dismantle the ship more easily for storing.

Mast assembly

If you study the drawing on page 30 you will see that the mast assembly is a very simple construction, consisting of two lengths of dowel rod fitted into two lengths of timber which brace the boat. This supports the mast – which is a broom handle!

I First make the mast support frame by drilling holes in the two pieces of timber for the dowel rods that go across the hull. Make two mast blocks and drill a hole in each at 90° in both planes (see page 93) for the cross-dowels and another one for the mast. Screw in a hook to hold the rigging handle. Push the cross-dowels through the mast blocks and glue the ends into the side pieces of timber. Glue the mast blocks in place in the centre of the cross-dowels.

2 Now make a block of wood to hold the rigging in place at the top of the mast. This must be drilled with a hole for the

mast and have two eyes screwed in position.

3 The sail is made from deck chair canvas which is available in pre-cut lengths (an expensive way to buy) or off the roll. Whether you choose nylon or cotton canvas, it is unlikely that it will be wide enough for the sail. I would strongly advise using double-sided carpet tape to join widths together, as I had a somewhat unfortunate encounter with a sewing machine on my first sail!

Once you have made the sail (sighs of relief!) tack the top edge to a batten of wood for the 'top yard'. Then fix the bottom edge (double-sided carpet tape again to the rescue!) to a length of plastic pipe such as overflow pipe, for the 'lower yard'.

4 Now – how to rig the sail. Thread a length of cord through the pipe and tie it to each side of the top dowel in the mast support frame.

Drill a hole at each end of the top yard. Thread another length of cord through these holes and knot it in position. To hold the sail to the mast and allow it to be raised and lowered, tie a third length of cord to the middle of the cord on the top yard. Thread it through the two eyes at the top of the mast and take it down to the cup hook on the upper mast block. Drill a hole through a short piece of dowel rod to form a handle and knot the end of the cord into this. When you take hold of the handle

and pull the cord out of the cup hook, the top yard drops down so lowering the sail. To raise the sail again, just pull the handle and loop the cord under the cup hook.

Final assembly

I Using lengths of cord, assemble the 'hull' by lacing the two sides together at the back (stern), and the sides and head post together at the prow. Don't be tempted to lace it too tight, otherwise the plywood will not bow sufficiently to get the mast assembly in place. Don't cut the cord to length until you're sure you've got it right. You can always trim bits off, but you can't stick them back on!

2 The shields hanging along the side of Viking boats were a very distinctive feature. To make these just draw circles out on plywood and cut them out using a jigsaw. Glasspaper the edges carefully. Cut out handles from timber using a compass with the specified radius to achieve the necessary curves. Glue the handles to the shields and add a screw from the other side for extra strength. I used striped plastic tape for decoration, but you can paint them in any way you wish, of course.

3 I painted lines along the length of the hull to simulate planks and a blue wavy line for the sea! Whatever you decide to do, follow the advice on page 95 on applying preservatives to give the ship protection against the sea and to prevent the growth of marine life!

Cutting list

Hull	2 off	2438 × 610 × 5mm (96 × 24 × ³/₁₆in)	Plywood
Head post	I off	1435 × 98 × 35mm (56½ × 3⅞ × 1⅜in)	Timber
Head	I off	584 × 356 × 9mm (23 × 14 × ⅜in)	Plywood
Teeth	Make from	610 × 51 × 22mm (24 × 2 × ⅞in)	Timber
Shield	8 off	356mm (14in) diam × 5mm (³/₁₆in)	Plywood
	8 off	152 × 95 × 9mm (6 × 3¾ × ⅜in)	Plywood
Mast support frame	2 off	406 × 76 × 22mm (16 × 3 × ⅞in)	Timber
	2 off	514mm (20¼in) × 20mm (¾in) diam dowelling	
Mast block	2 off	152 × 95 × 35mm (6 × 3¾ × 1⅜in)	Timber
Mast	I off	1676mm (66in) × 20mm (¾in) diam dowelling	
	I off	114 × 95 × 35mm (4½ × 3¾ × 1⅜in)	Timber
Top yard	I off	1054 × 28 × 22mm (41½ × 1⅛ × ⅞in)	Timber
Sail hoisting handle	I off	146mm (5¾in) × 20mm (¾in) diam dowelling	
Eyes	2 off	89 × 38 × 22mm (3½ × 1½ × ⅞in)	Timber

Ancillaries

	I off	915mm (36in) wide × 1525mm (60in) long nylon deckchair canvas	
	I off	5.50 metres (18ft) strong nylon cord	
	I off	991mm (39in) × 22mm (⅞in) °/diam plastic water waste pipe	
	2 off	25mm (1in) screwed eyes	
	I off	25mm (1in) screwed hook	

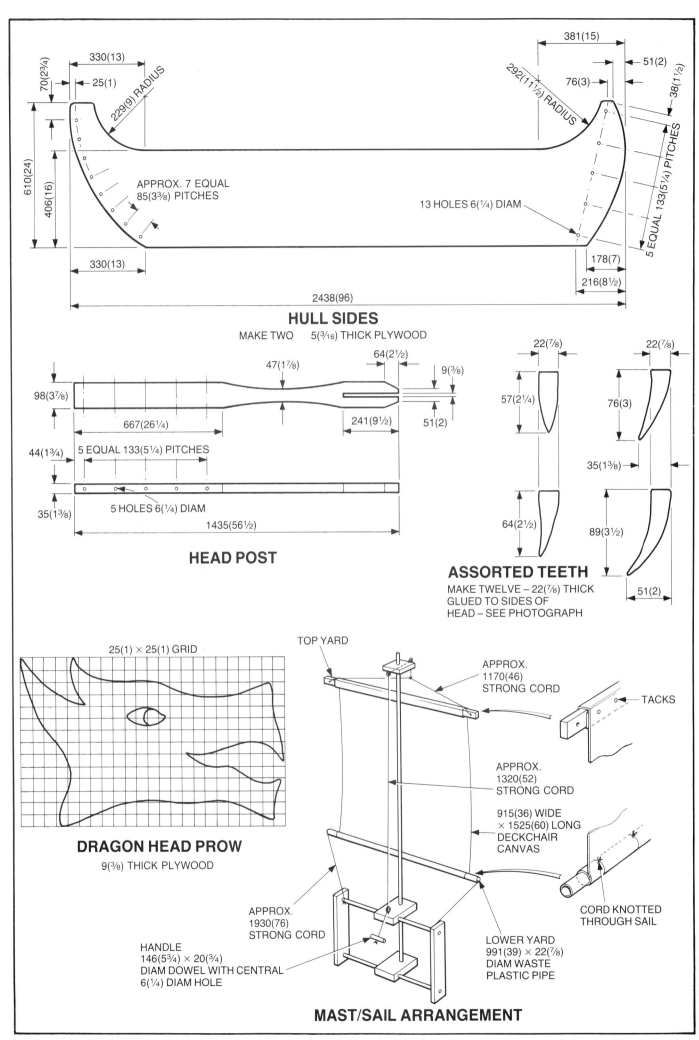

330(13)
25(1)
70(2¾)
229(9) RADIUS
610(24)
406(16)
330(13)
APPROX. 7 EQUAL
85(3⅜) PITCHES
2438(96)

381(15)
51(2)
292(11½) RADIUS
76(3)
38(1½)
5 EQUAL 133(5¼) PITCHES
13 HOLES 6(¼) DIAM
178(7)
216(8½)

HULL SIDES

MAKE TWO   5(³⁄₁₆) THICK PLYWOOD

98(3⅞)
47(1⅞)
64(2½)
9(⅜)
241(9½)
51(2)
667(26¼)
44(1¾)
5 EQUAL 133(5¼) PITCHES
35(1⅜)
5 HOLES 6(¼) DIAM
1435(56½)

HEAD POST

22(⅞)
22(⅞)
57(2¼)
76(3)
35(1⅜)
64(2½)
89(3½)
51(2)

ASSORTED TEETH

MAKE TWELVE – 22(⅞) THICK
GLUED TO SIDES OF
HEAD – SEE PHOTOGRAPH

25(1) × 25(1) GRID

DRAGON HEAD PROW

9(⅜) THICK PLYWOOD

TOP YARD
APPROX.
1170(46)
STRONG CORD
TACKS

APPROX.
1320(52)
STRONG CORD

915(36) WIDE
× 1525(60) LONG
DECKCHAIR
CANVAS

APPROX.
1930(76)
STRONG CORD

CORD KNOTTED
THROUGH SAIL

HANDLE
146(5¾) × 20(¾)
DIAM DOWEL WITH CENTRAL
6(¼) DIAM HOLE

LOWER YARD
991(39) × 22(⅞)
DIAM WASTE
PLASTIC PIPE

MAST/SAIL ARRANGEMENT

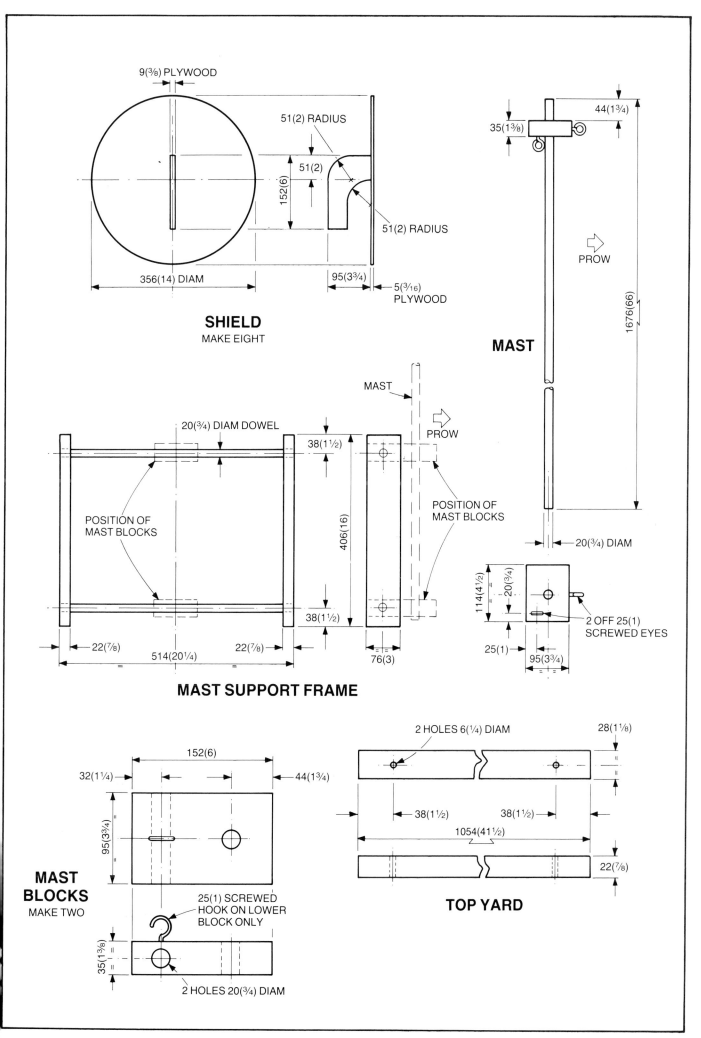

9(⅜) PLYWOOD

51(2) RADIUS

51(2)

152(6)

51(2) RADIUS

356(14) DIAM

95(3¾)

5(³⁄₁₆)
PLYWOOD

SHIELD
MAKE EIGHT

35(1⅜)

44(1¾)

PROW

1676(66)

MAST

20(¾) DIAM

20(¾) DIAM DOWEL

38(1½)

MAST

PROW

POSITION OF
MAST BLOCKS

POSITION OF
MAST BLOCKS

406(16)

38(1½)

22(⅞)

22(⅞)

514(20¼)

76(3)

114(4½)

20(¾)

25(1)

95(3¾)

2 OFF 25(1)
SCREWED EYES

MAST SUPPORT FRAME

152(6)

32(1¼)

44(1¾)

95(3¾)

**MAST
BLOCKS**
MAKE TWO

25(1) SCREWED
HOOK ON LOWER
BLOCK ONLY

35(1⅜)

2 HOLES 20(¾) DIAM

2 HOLES 6(¼) DIAM

28(1⅛)

38(1½)

38(1½)

1054(41½)

22(⅞)

TOP YARD

31

DUMP TRUCK

Children love toys that are capable of carrying building bricks, sand and, if you are lucky, logs for the fire or lawn cuttings for the compost heap! So, to aid the garden work-force I have designed this simple dump truck which I hope will be eagerly used by all aspiring transport managers. It will provide tremendous play value and is not too difficult or time-consuming to make.

The chassis and seat are made from Nordic redwood and the tipper from Finnish plywood.

1 Start with the chassis. Cut the main plank to length and mark out a groove at one end to take the steel rod that will hold the tipper body to the chassis. This arrangement is far stronger than using hinges which would not stand up to the hours of wear and tear the truck will get.

The groove does not have to be round. All you have to do is cut a trench of sufficient depth to hold the steel axe firmly, and there are a number of ways of doing this. You can use: a tenon saw to cut along the edges and remove the

waste with a chisel; a traditional plough plane (see page 94); an electric router – if you have access to one of these wonderful power tools. The most important thing is to ensure that the trench is cut to a uniform width and depth. Keep laying the steel axle in the groove as you work on it to check the fit.

Once you have finished this trench you have to cut an identical one in another piece of wood. This will form the 'lid' of the axle channel and hold it in position on the chassis plank. I found it

Market stall

easier to do this on the end of a longer plank and then cut off the strip I needed. When you have done this, round off one of the top edges of the strip as shown on the plans and screw it on to the end of the chassis plank, driving the screws in from underneath the chassis.

2   In order to prevent little fingers getting trapped under the tipper body when it is closed, you need to glue and screw a strip of wood across the chassis plank and fit some large rubber buffer pads on top. You could use a number of tap washers held to the mounting block with a screw through the middle if you can't find any suitable pads.

3   Cut out the mounting block for the castors at the back, drill holes for these and then glue and screw the block to the underside of the chassis plank.

4   Now make the seat. Cut out the four pieces of timber required (back, sides and seat). I gave the side pieces angles to add a realistic look to the 'engine compartment'. The back must have the corners rounded off for safety reasons – use a chisel or spokeshave for this job and glasspaper it well. I strongly advise counterboring all the screws as screw heads can scratch and spoil the look of the finished toy (see page 93). Plug the

holes with dowel rod glued into place, the excess cut off and the surface glasspapered smooth.

5   Now make the catch that holds the tipper body in the closed position. It is essential to make this from plywood which has none of the short-grain weaknesses of ordinary timber. Mark the shape out carefully and then cut it out using a coping saw. Cut out the mounting block and cut the slot for the catch to fit into using a tenon saw for the vertical cuts and a' coping saw to remove the waste piece. The catch should fit tightly into the mounting block, but still allow movement. With the catch in position, drill the hole for the dowel rod that will hold it there. Screw the mounting block on to the underside of the seat and fit the catch and dowel rod in position.

6   Screw the entire seat assembly on to the chassis by passing screws from the underside of the chassis plank into the sides of the seat.

7   Mark and cut out the two sides, back, front and floor of the tipper body from a sheet of plywood. Tape the sides together and drill holes for the dowel rod that the catch hooks on to, and also for the steel axle at the bottom.
Glue and screw the tipper body

together using glue and 'superscrews' as these have threads that are better suited to fixing plywood than those of ordinary screws. You will find it helpful to have the dowel rod and steel axle in place whilst you carry out this stage.

8   Now you are ready to fix the tipper on to the chassis. Thread the steel axle through the tipper sides into the channel you made at the front of the chassis plank and out through the other side, placing a piece of plastic tubing on either side between the tipper sides and chassis plank to act as spacers and keep the tipper body in the centre of the chassis.

9   Fix wheels and spring caps on the ends of the axle (see page 94) and screw two castors on to the back of the truck. Castors make the toy very manoeuvrable.

10   Finish off the toy with a good glasspapering and see page 95 for advice on wood preservatives and exterior paints. As you can see from the photograph on page 49, I also added some brightly coloured tape for extra decoration. Pay particular attention to painting the inside of the tipper as this will have to withstand sand and logs being loaded in with great vigour!

Cutting list

Chassis assembly	1 off	527 × 194 × 20mm (20¾ × 7⅝ × ¾in)	Timber
	2 off	194 × 44 × 20mm (7⅝ × 1¾ × ¾in)	Timber
	1 off	254 × 67 × 20mm (10 × 2⅝ × ¾in)	Timber
	1 off	152 × 95 × 20mm (6 × 3¾ × ¾in)	Timber
Seat assembly	1 off	254 × 194 × 20mm (10 × 7⅝ × ¾in)	Timber
	2 off	254 × 95 × 20mm (10 × 3¾ × ¾in)	Timber
	1 off	194 × 95 × 20mm (7⅝ × 3¾ × ¾in)	Timber
Catch	1 off	229 × 83 × 9mm (9 × 3¼ × ⅜in)	Plywood
Catch mounting block assembly	1 off	127 × 95 × 20mm (5 × 3¾ × ¾in)	Timber
	1 off	95mm (3¾in) × 9mm (⅜in) diam dowelling	
Tipper body – sides	2 off	381 × 305 × 9mm (15 × 12 × ⅜in)	Plywood
– front and back	2 off	302 × 203 × 9mm (11⅞ × 8 × ⅜in)	Plywood
– floor	1 off	302 × 235 × 9mm (11⅞ × 9¼ × ⅜in)	Plywood
– handle	1 off	330mm (13in) × 16mm (⅝in) diam dowelling	

Ancillaries

	2 off	197mm (7¾in) diam road wheels	
	2 off	12mm (½in) spring dome caps	
	2 off	20mm (¾in) °/diam × 12mm (½in) ¹/diam	
		× 54mm (2⅛in) spacers	
	1 off	432mm (17in) × 12mm (½in) diam steel axle	
	2 off	51mm (2in) diam castoring wheel assemblies	
	3 off	12mm (½in) diam × 12mm (½in) high rubber buffer pads	

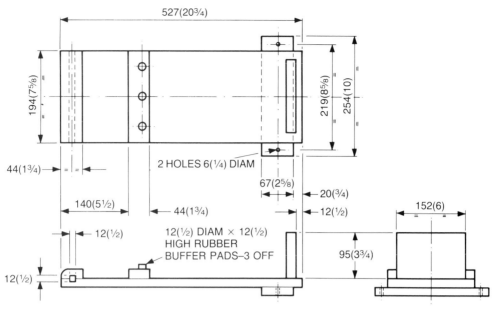

CHASSIS ASSEMBLY
20(¾) THICK TIMBER

527(20¾)

194(7⅝)

219(8⅝)

254(10)

2 HOLES 6(¼) DIAM

44(1¾)

140(5½)

44(1¾)

67(2⅝)

20(¾)

12(½)

12(½)

12(½) DIAM × 12(½)
HIGH RUBBER
BUFFER PADS–3 OFF

95(3¾)

152(6)

12(½)

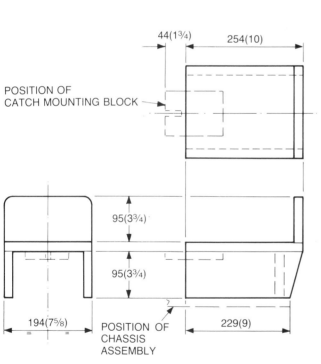

44(1¾)

254(10)

POSITION OF
CATCH MOUNTING BLOCK

95(3¾)

95(3¾)

194(7⅝)

POSITION OF
CHASSIS
ASSEMBLY

229(9)

SEAT ASSEMBLY
20(¾) THICK

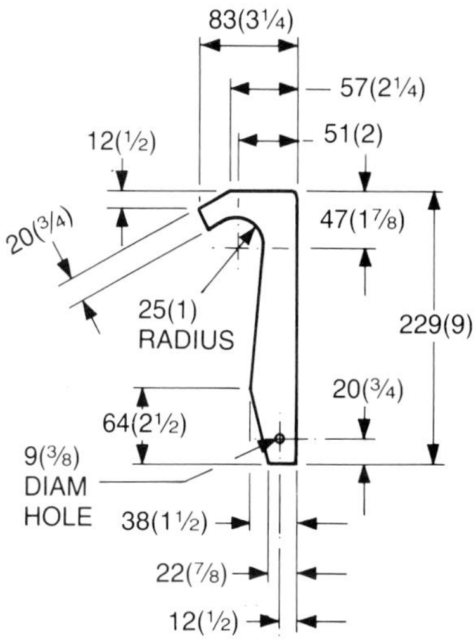

83(3¼)

57(2¼)

51(2)

12(½)

20(¾)

25(1)
RADIUS

47(1⅞)

229(9)

20(¾)

64(2½)

9(⅜)
DIAM
HOLE

38(1½)

22(⅞)

12(½)

CATCH
9(⅜) THICK PLYWOOD

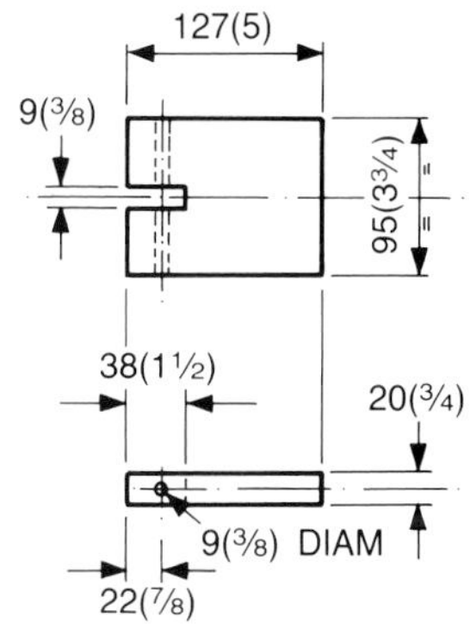

127(5)

9(⅜)

95(3¾)

38(1½)

20(¾)

9(⅜) DIAM

22(⅞)

CATCH MOUNTING BLOCK

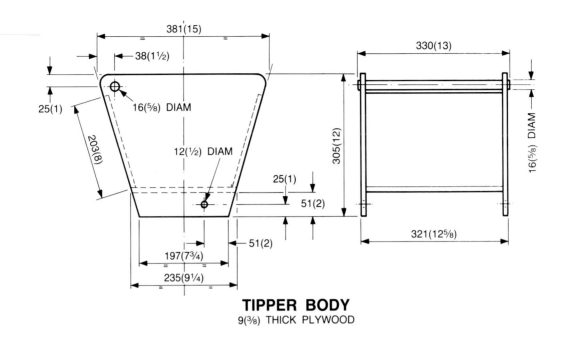

TIPPER BODY
9(³⁄₈) THICK PLYWOOD

Trojan horse

Children love to imitate things from the 'real world.' This truck gives a child somewhere to put different size parcels and letters for playing 'postman' and can also be used to store books and toys. To avoid the problem of pinched fingers and broken hinges I used magnetic catches such as are used to keep fitted-cupboards doors shut, to hold the side door in place.

The axles and handle assembly are made from Nordic redwood and the body is made from plywood.

Handle and axles

1 First make the front and back axle blocks that hold the wheels and steel axles in place. Mark out the shape on your timber including the curved centre portion (see page 42). Carefully cut out each block, using a coping saw to remove the curved piece.

2 Drill the holes to take the steel axles, being careful to keep the drill at 90° in both planes (see page 93). On the front axle block, mark and cut out the halving joint (see page 90) that is needed to accommodate the hitch bar for the towing handle.

3 Mark and cut out the hitch bar. Drill the hole to take the dowel that attaches it to the towing handle. Then mark and cut out the second stage of the halving joint you started on the front axle block.

Finally, mark out the slot for the towing handle. Cut down both sides with a tenon saw, then use a coping saw to cut the waste piece off at the base. As I

explain on page 91, the coping saw frame can be swivelled at different angles to the blade which makes it an ideal tool for this sort of job.

4   Now for the handle itself. Start by marking and cutting out the basic shape.

You now have to work on the handle to give it an attractive and smooth shape and there are a variety of tools you can use to do this (see page 91). Whatever you decide to use, do be certain that you remove all sharp edges and any possibility of splinters.

5   Check that the handle fits snugly into its slot in the hitch bar. Work on the pieces with glasspaper, if necessary, to get a comfortable fit.

Holding the handle in place (a helper is very useful here), drill through the hitch bar and handle in one operation, keeping the drill at 90° in both planes (see page 93), to create the hole needed for the dowel rod pin.

Cut the dowel rod to length and glue it in place (see page 92) so that the handle is firmly attached to the hitch bar. Make sure that no surplus glue gets on to the handle and dowel rod, otherwise the handle will not move freely.

6   As the wheels are tucked under the body, spacer blocks of wood are needed to give them adequate clearance. Simply glue and screw the back wooden axle block on to its spacer block and, at a later stage, glue (and/or screw) it on to the van base.

7   The front axle is slightly different as it is designed to swivel for comfortable manoeuvring up and down garden paths. For this reason it is attached to its spacer

and the base by means of a coach bolt (see page 94).

Tape the spacer and front axle together and drill the hole for the coach bolt. Now separate them and counterbore the hole in the top of the spacer (see page 93) so that the head of the coach bolt will be flush with the wood, enabling you to glue and/or screw the spacer to the underside of the van base. Assemble the front axle, spacer and coach bolt, using a washer under the nut, and when you have done the nut up tight, 'burr over' – i.e. blunt the thread – with a hammer to prevent it coming undone.

The body

The chassis of the van is basically four pieces of plywood glued together, with compartments inside. Do make sure you mark and cut out all the sides and partitions accurately – otherwise you'll have terrible trouble when you come to glue them all up.

1   Read the note on page 91 about cutting plywood, then carefully mark and cut out all the chassis pieces required.

2   Clamp the roof, floor, front and rear pieces together in the correct position to check for fit. You can either use very large 'G' clamps for this or the Stanley Webb strap (see page 92). If all is well, glue the chassis together and, while the glue is still wet, check it is 'square' by placing a dowel rod diagonally from corner to corner. Make pencil marks on the rod where the corners are. Then place it across the other diagonal and gently adjust the plywood chassis until the corners and pencil marks line up.

As plywood only gives you a thin

glueing edge, you may find it easier to fix the sides on with plastic corner blocks instead. There is a variety on the market and they are very easy to use.

3   Now fit the interior partitions. You don't, of course, have to follow my choice of dividers, but however many you decide to fit, do cut them out accurately and glue them carefully in place.

4   Fix four magnetic catches – one in each corner of the body – to hold the door in place. Mark and cut out the two grab handles, and then shape them with a spokeshave (page 91) till you have nice rounded edges. Glue the handles in position at each end of the door.

5   I also cut out and shaped two pieces of timber for the roof. These are optional, but when glued in place at the back and front do add to the character of the finished toy. Also, because I rounded them off with a spokeshave, they are safer than the sharp corners of the plywood chassis.

Final assembly and finishing

1   Glue the wooden spacers which you have already fixed to the axle blocks to the underside of the van chassis. You can add screws for extra strength.

2   Now you are ready to finish with polyurethane varnish – I use three coats to get a really good result, but do not leave this toy outside for the reasons explained on page 95. The red GPO logos add an extra special touch.

3   Finally, fit the steel axles and wheels (see page 94).

Cutting list

Body panels	Make from	1524 × 610 × 9mm (60 × 24 × 3/8in)	Plywood
Axle blocks	2 off	254 × 67 × 38mm (10 × 25/8 × 1 1/2in)	Timber
Spacer blocks	2 off	222 × 67 × 38mm (83/4 × 25/8 × 1 1/2in)	Timber
Hitch bar	1 off	229 × 67 × 32mm (9 × 25/8 × 1 1/4in)	Timber
Handle	1 off	502 × 70 × 22mm (193/4 × 23/4 × 7/8in)	Timber
Roof shaping	2 off	305 × 47 × 22mm (12 × 17/8 × 7/8in)	Timber
Grab handles	2 off	508 × 47 × 22mm (20 × 17/8 × 7/8in)	Timber
Hitch pin	1 off	67mm (25/8in) × 16mm (5/8in) diam dowelling	

Ancillaries

	4 off	159mm (61/4in) diam road wheels	
	2 off	318mm (121/2in) × 9mm (3/8in) diam steel axles	
	2 off	9mm (3/8in) spring dome caps	
	1 off	76mm (3in) × 6mm (1/4in) coach bolt and nut	
	2 off	6mm (1/4in) 'penny' washers	
	4 off	Magnetic catches	

Volvo shovel-loader

Viking longboat

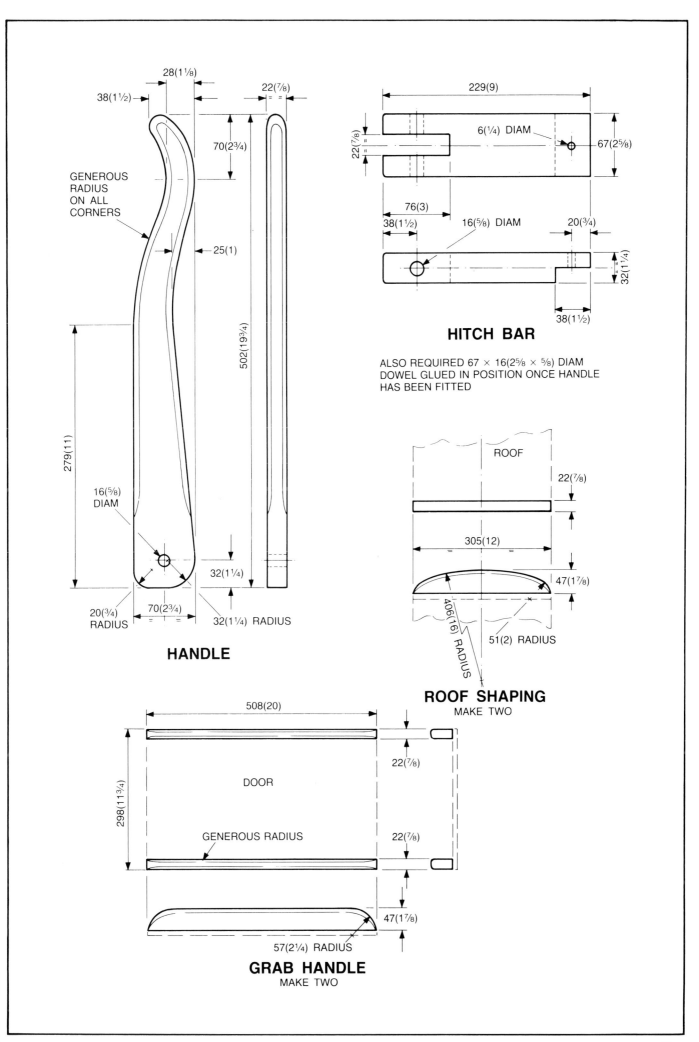

28(1⅛)

38(1½)

22(⅞)

70(2¾)

GENEROUS
RADIUS
ON ALL
CORNERS

25(1)

502(19¾)

279(11)

16(⅝)
DIAM

32(1¼)

20(¾)
RADIUS

70(2¾)

32(1¼) RADIUS

HANDLE

229(9)

22(⅞)

6(¼) DIAM

67(2⅝)

76(3)

16(⅝) DIAM

20(¾)

38(1½)

32(1¼)

38(1½)

HITCH BAR

ALSO REQUIRED 67 × 16(2⅝ × ⅝) DIAM
DOWEL GLUED IN POSITION ONCE HANDLE
HAS BEEN FITTED

ROOF

22(⅞)

305(12)

47(1⅞)

406(16) RADIUS

51(2) RADIUS

ROOF SHAPING
MAKE TWO

508(20)

22(⅞)

DOOR

298(11¾)

22(⅞)

GENEROUS RADIUS

47(1⅞)

57(2¼) RADIUS

GRAB HANDLE
MAKE TWO

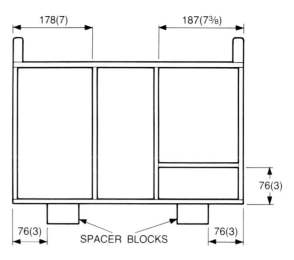

178(7)   187(7³⁄₈)

76(3)

76(3)   SPACER BLOCKS   76(3)

BODY ARRANGEMENT

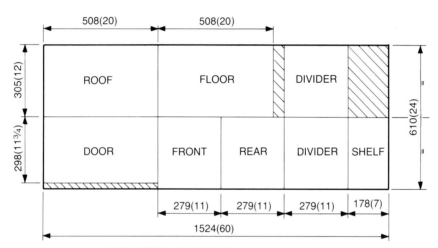

508(20)   508(20)

305(12)

298(11³⁄₄)

| ROOF | FLOOR | DIVIDER |
| DOOR | FRONT | REAR | DIVIDER | SHELF |

610(24)

279(11)   279(11)   279(11)   178(7)

1524(60)

SUGGESTED LAYOUT OF PANELS FROM
A SHEET OF 9(³⁄₈) THICK PLYWOOD

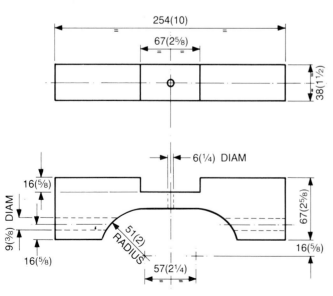

254(10)

67(2⁵⁄₈)

38(1¹⁄₂)

6(¹⁄₄) DIAM

16(⁵⁄₈)

9(³⁄₈) DIAM

16(⁵⁄₈)

51(2) RADIUS

67(2⁵⁄₈)

16(⁵⁄₈)

57(2¹⁄₄)

AXLE BLOCK
MAKE TWO

CENTRAL HOLE & HALVING JOINT CUTOUT
REQUIRED ONLY IN THE FRONT BLOCK

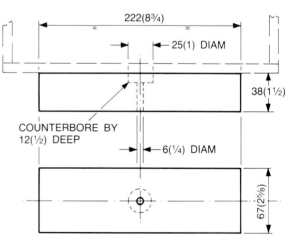

222(8³⁄₄)

25(1) DIAM

38(1¹⁄₂)

COUNTERBORE BY
12(¹⁄₂) DEEP

6(¹⁄₄) DIAM

67(2⁵⁄₈)

SPACER BLOCK
MAKE TWO

CENTRAL HOLE REQUIRED ONLY
IN THE FRONT BLOCK

VOLVO SHOVEL LOADER

This shovel loader is the ideal machine for large contract digging in the sand pit! The front scoop can be raised and lowered by a large lever which is conveniently placed for the driver's hand and the bucket can be swivelled and locked into position when loads of sand have to be transported off site.

It is fairly simple to make and will withstand all the rigours of child play in the great outdoors. I used Nordic redwood in stock sizes for the job.

1 Mark and cut out the two body side panels. Tape them together and mark and cut out the recessed section for the operator's cab. Drill the holes for the wheel axles. Separate the panels and drill pilot holes for the bucket arms (both sides) and the bucket lever (right-hand panel only).

2 The body panels are held together by pieces of timber (infill panels) glued between their inside faces. Cut out the five infill panels required. Cramp up the

body of the vehicle 'dry' to check everything fits (see page 92), then separate the pieces, apply glue and cramp them in position again. You will probably find it helpful to thread the steel axles in position to help keep everything lined up while the glue is drying. Do check that the chassis is square when you have tightened the cramps as the glue will make things slip.

3 Now cut out the four strips for the 'radiator panel' at the back of the shovel

loader. Glue these into position when the glue has set on the main body. You could add further detailing by panel-pinning strips of aluminium mesh between the grille bars.

4　The cab is the next job to tackle. Make a template out of cardboard (see page 90) for the side walls and use it to mark them out onto your timber. Before you cut them out, however, cut a rebate along the bottom edge of the timber. This will enable you to position the side walls on to the body more easily. Now cut out the side walls and remove the waste piece in the middle for the cab window using a jigsaw or coping saw. Use glasspaper to achieve a good finish and round off the corners at the bottom of the windows.

5　Cut out the other pieces needed for the cab: the three cross members and rear cab wall that will hold the side walls together; the seat; and the roof. You also need to make the console assembly. For this you need to drill a hole in a disc of thick dowelling rod and glue a piece of thinner dowelling into this hole to form the steering wheel. Cut out and shape a block of timber (note the angle needed at the bottom), drill a hole of the appropriate diameter and glue the steering wheel in position.

　Pay particular attention to all the edges of the cab pieces. Make sure they are all rounded off nicely and smoothed with glasspaper, especially the roof. When they are ready for fitting, cramp the cab together dry to check everything fits and then glue the cross members and rear cab wall in position, checking that the cramps are holding it square while the glue dries. Then glue the seat and console in place and, finally, glue on the roof.

　You can add more detail by glueing small plywood or dowelling 'instrument' discs to the inside of the lower windscreen, if you wish.

6　Now make the rear mudguards. These are rather 'over-size' for the scale of the toy, the reason being that a youngster not only needs a wide 'platform' to sit on, but also protection from the wheels.

　The only difficult bit of this job is the angle that is needed at the top of the upright sections. Mark the angle carefully (see page 90) and use a smoothing plane (see page 94) to remove the waste,

working from both sides into the centre. Your plane will need to be very sharp as you are cutting across the grain.

The Bucket

The bucket is made from plywood. Get Finnish plywood if you can as it is very good quality.

1　Make a template for the sides, following the dimensions given on the plans. Draw round it on to your plywood and cut out the two sides using a jigsaw (see page 91). Drill holes for the steel rod that will hold the bucket to the arms.

2　Cut to length the back of the bucket which is made from stock size timber. Glue the bucket sides and bottom on to this piece of timber.

3　Cut out the pieces of timber that fit on to the plywood bottom of the bucket and on to the top edge of the timber back, between the plywood sides. The former should have a chamfered edge to aid sand scooping. Glue them in position.

4　The plywood sides need strengthening where the steel rod that attaches the bucket to the arms is fixed. Cut out two semi-circular pieces of timber and drill holes for the rod. Glue them in position on the inside faces of the sides, behind the back of the bucket.

5　Now make the bucket handle. This involves a certain amount of shaping as there are two curved sections. Once you have marked out your curves in pencil, use a jigsaw or coping saw to remove the waste. Drill the hole for the steel rod that will attach it to the bucket.

7　Now make the locking lever and lock pin that control the tilting of the bucket. Drill a hole in the lever to take the lock pin (which is simply one piece of dowelling glued into another piece). The locking lever now has to be glued and screwed on to the inside of the left-hand bucket side.

8　The bucket is held to the body of the shovel loader by means of two parallel arms. At the body end they are screwed in place and at the bucket end they are held in position by a steel rod. Make the two arms and drill holes for the steel rod and the necessary screws.

　You also need to drill a hole in the left-hand arm for the lock pin. To make sure this aligns properly, line up the arms

with the sides and thread the steel rod in position. Cover the end of the lock pin with pencil or chalk. Holding the locking lever parallel to the left-hand arm, push the lock pin through the hole in the locking lever and turn it against the arm.

　Take everything apart again and the lead graphite from the pencil, or the chalk dust, on the bucket arm will show you where to drill your hole for the lock pin. When the toy is finally in use, the lock pin will be pushed in and out of these holes to lock and unlock the bucket.

　Glue and screw a cross piece of timber in place on the underside of the bucket arms to hold them parallel.

　Finally, screw the bucket arm assembly onto the sides of the shovel loader body using very large gauge screws (No. 8–12) for strength. It is a good idea to fit a cup screw, if you can get one large enough, or a washer under the screw head.

9　Now cut out and shape the lever that controls the raising and lowering of the bucket. Drill the holes for the screws that will attach it to the body panel. The screws you use should again be large gauge (No. 8–12) with a washer or a cup screw under the head. When the lever is pulled up, the end will press down on the end of the bucket arm and raise the bucket. Tighten the screw that attaches the lever to the body panel enough for it to hold a bucket of sand securely in the raised position.

10　Thread the steel rod through the sides of the bucket, the arms and the bucket handle using two lengths of plastic tubing as spacers, one each side of the handle, to ensure the arms stay in place.

11　A good glass papering all over and several coats of non-toxic varnish will finish the toy off properly, but do not leave the toy outside for long for the reasons explained on page 95. Volvo logos are available from 'Wheels'.

12　The final job is to fit the axles, wheels and spring caps. To give the impression of the huge width of tyre used by Volvo on such trucks I used two wheels on each side. The ones at the back have to be held clear of the chassis sides by two lengths of plastic tubing. I painted the wheel centres and the ends of the handle and operating lever rod red to give it a dash of colour.

Mail truck

Cutting list

Body side panel	2 off	533 × 191 × 22mm (21 × 7½ × ⅞in)	Timber
Infill panels	1 off	283 × 95 × 22mm (11⅛ × 3¾ × ⅞in)	Timber
	1 off	270 × 95 × 22mm (10⅝ × 3¾ × ⅞in)	Timber
	1 off	197 × 95 × 22mm (7¾ × 3¾ × ⅞in)	Timber
	1 off	168 × 95 × 22mm (6⅝ × 3¾ × ⅞in)	Timber
	1 off	140 × 95 × 22mm (5½ × 3¾ × ⅞in)	Timber
Radiator grille bars	4 off	95 × 16 × 6mm (3¾ × ⅝ × ¼in)	Timber
Mudguards	2 off	184 × 79 × 22mm (7¼ × 3⅛ × ⅞in)	Timber
	2 off	152 × 79 × 22mm (6 × 3⅛ × ⅞in)	Timber
Cab side wall	2 off	191 × 165 × 22mm (7½ × 6½ × ⅞in)	Timber
Roof	1 off	178 × 178 × 22mm (7 × 7 × ⅞in)	Timber
Upper windscreen cross member	1 off	152 × 32 × 22mm (6 × 1¼ × ⅞in)	Timber
Lower windscreen cross member	1 off	152 × 44 × 22mm (6 × 1¾ × ⅞in)	Timber
Rear window upper cross member	1 off	114 × 32 × 22mm (4½ × 1¼ × ⅞in)	Timber
Rear cab wall	1 off	114 × 70 × 22mm (4½ × 2¾ × ⅞in)	Timber
Seat	1 off	114 × 54 × 22mm (4½ × 2⅛ × ⅞in)	Timber
Console assembly	1 off	60 × 47 × 22mm (2⅜ × 1⅞ × ⅞in)	Timber
	1 off	32 × 32 × 6mm (1¼ × 1¼ × ¼in)	Timber
	1 off	38mm (1½in) × 6mm (¼in) diam dowelling	
Bucket handle	1 off	254 × 70 × 22mm (10 × 2¾ × ⅞in)	Timber
Lever to raise bucket	1 off	264 × 44 × 22mm (10⅜ × 1¾ × ⅞in)	Timber
Lock lever	1 off	152 × 47 × 22mm (6 × 1⅞ × ⅞in)	Timber
Lock pin	1 off	89mm (3½in) × 20mm (¾in) diam dowelling	
	1 off	102mm (4in) × 9mm (⅜in) diam dowelling	
Bucket arm assembly	2 off	381 × 47 × 22mm (15 × 1⅞ × ⅞in)	Timber
	1 off	184 × 47 × 22mm (7¼ × 1⅞ × ⅞in)	Timber
Bucket	1 off	330 × 152 × 22mm (13 × 6 × ⅞in)	Timber
	1 off	349 × 133 × 9mm (13¾ × 5¼ × ⅜in)	Plywood
	1 off	349 × 57 × 9mm (13¾ × 2¼ × ⅜in)	Timber
	2 off	149 × 159 × 9mm (5⅞ × 6¼ × ⅜in)	Plywood
	2 off	159 × 54 × 22mm (6¼ × 2⅛ × ⅞in)	Timber
	1 off	330 × 25 × 6mm (13 × 1 × ¼in)	Timber

Ancillaries

	8 off	152mm (6in) diam road wheels
	2 off	343mm (13½in) × 9mm (⅜in) diam steel rods
	4 off	9mm (⅜in) spring dome caps
	4 off	20mm (¾in) × 9mm (⅜in) i/diam plastic tube spacers
	1 off	362mm (14¼in) × 6mm (¼in) diam steel rod
	2 off	6mm (¼in) spring dome caps
	2 off	57mm (2¼in) × 6mm (¼in) i/diam plastic tube spacers

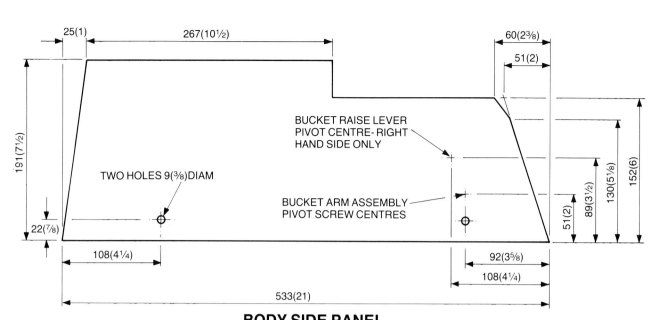

BODY SIDE PANEL
MAKE TWO   22(⅞) THICK TIMBER

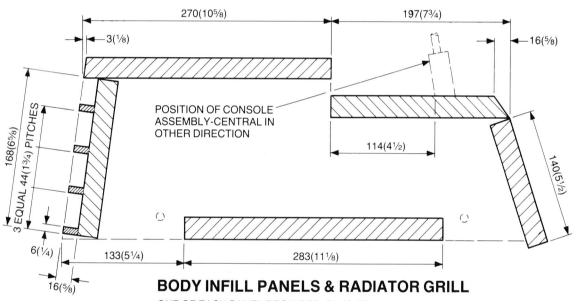

BODY INFILL PANELS & RADIATOR GRILL
ONE OF EACH PANEL REQUIRED, PLUS FOUR GRILL BARS.
PANEL 22(⅞) THICK TIMBER, GRILLE BARS 6(¼) THICK TIMBER-
ALL 95(3¾) WIDE

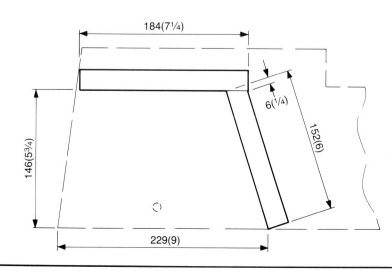

REAR MUDGUARD
MAKE TWO PAIRS
22(⅞) THICK TIMBER × 79(3⅛) WIDE

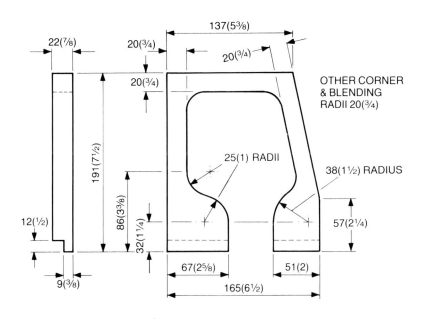

CAB SIDE WALL
MAKE TWO   ONE OF EACH HAND

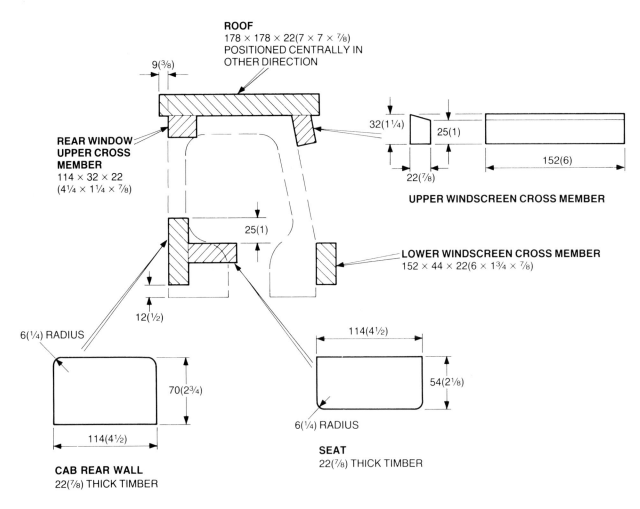

ROOF
178 × 178 × 22(7 × 7 × 7/8)
POSITIONED CENTRALLY IN
OTHER DIRECTION

REAR WINDOW
UPPER CROSS
MEMBER
114 × 32 × 22
(4¼ × 1¼ × 7/8)

UPPER WINDSCREEN CROSS MEMBER

LOWER WINDSCREEN CROSS MEMBER
152 × 44 × 22(6 × 1¾ × 7/8)

6(¼) RADIUS

6(¼) RADIUS

CAB REAR WALL
22(7/8) THICK TIMBER

SEAT
22(7/8) THICK TIMBER

CAB ASSEMBLY

48

Garden house

Dump truck

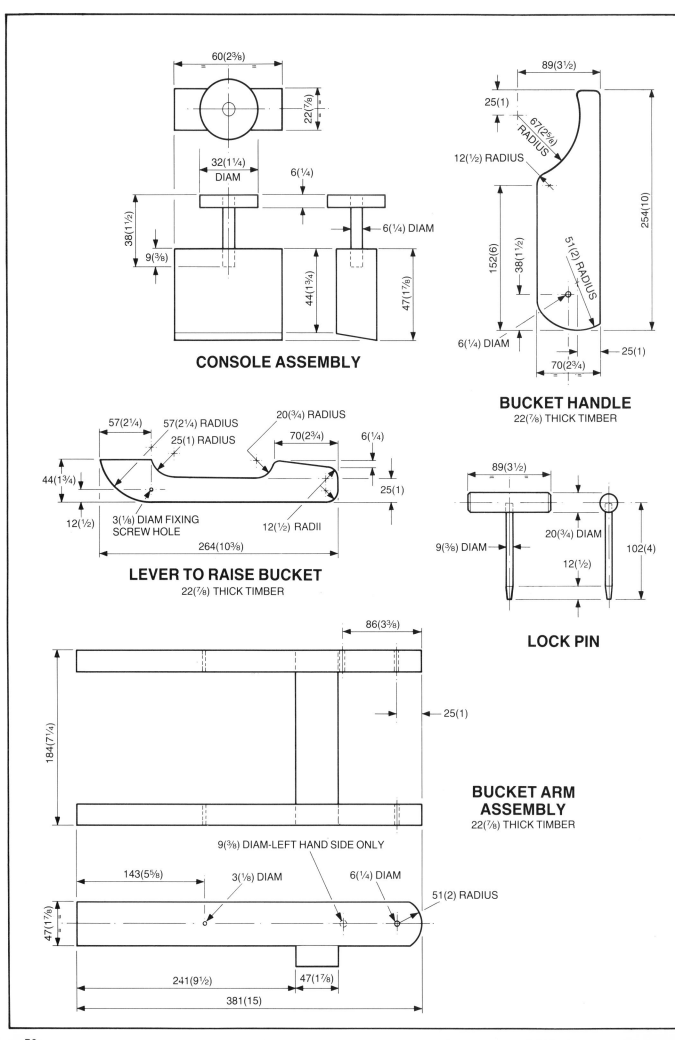

CONSOLE ASSEMBLY

BUCKET HANDLE
22(⅞) THICK TIMBER

LEVER TO RAISE BUCKET
22(⅞) THICK TIMBER

LOCK PIN

BUCKET ARM ASSEMBLY
22(⅞) THICK TIMBER

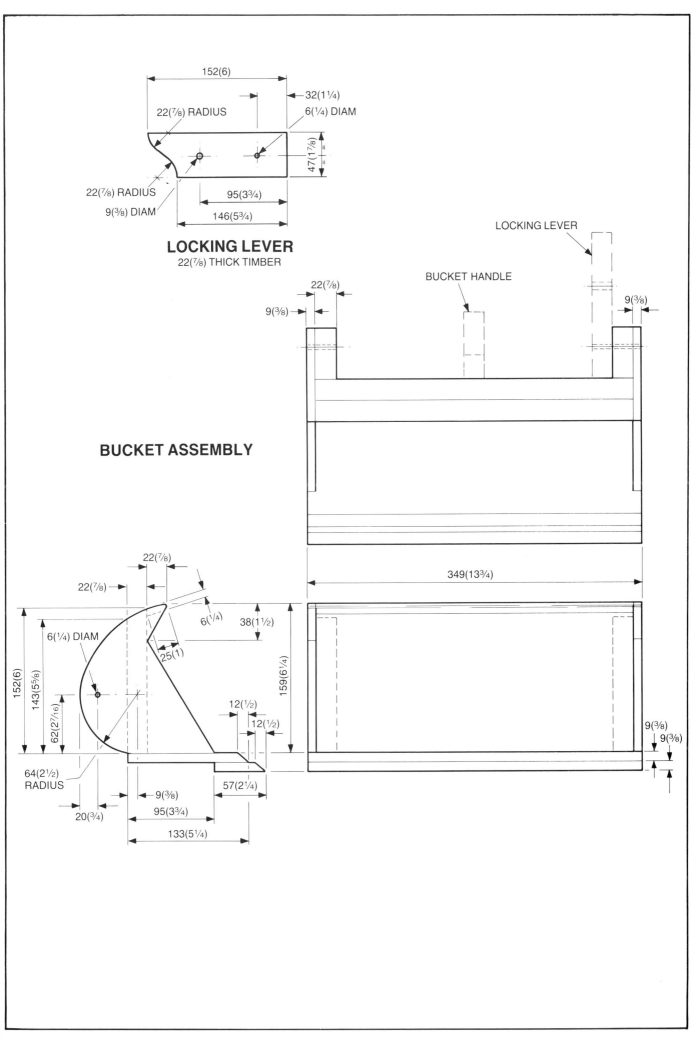

152(6)

32(1¼)

22(⅞) RADIUS

6(¼) DIAM

47(1⅞)

22(⅞) RADIUS

9(⅜) DIAM

95(3¾)

146(5¾)

LOCKING LEVER
22(⅞) THICK TIMBER

LOCKING LEVER

BUCKET HANDLE

22(⅞)

9(⅜)

9(⅜)

BUCKET ASSEMBLY

349(13¾)

22(⅞)

22(⅞)

6(¼)

38(1½)

6(¼) DIAM

25(1)

152(6)

143(5⅝)

62(2⁷⁄₁₆)

159(6¼)

12(½)

12(½)

9(⅜)

9(⅜)

64(2½)
RADIUS

9(⅜)

57(2¼)

20(¾)

95(3¾)

133(5¼)

CASTLE

'A horse, a horse, my kingdom for a horse.' In retrospect it might have done Richard III more good if he had asked for a castle! These defensive medieval buildings are found throughout the country, and exploring the dark, dank passages, the scary heights of the look-out towers, the primitive living conditions and the dungeons where the prisoners were held makes you glad that you live in the twentieth century.

This castle, I am glad to say is a far more friendly building and gives great scope for playing 'baddies and goodies'. It is made entirely from standard plywood sheets held together by wooden battens, and you can adapt the towers and walls to suit your garden or play area. For stability, it is best to arrange for a tower to be at the end of each wall section.

If you decide to make wooden swords, they need to be carefully rounded off and you should fit large lumps of Blu-tack on the ends of the dowel-rod arrows. The bows I made from standard battens, free from knots and planed down and bound the centres with plastic tape. The bows and arrows need to be used with adult supervision and on no account should the bows be made capable of firing anything heavy or pointed. The bows detailed in the drawings were capable of shooting some 40 feet – quite sufficient! Do emphasise to your children that they must take great care with 'weapons'.

Before you tackle the project read the advice on pages 91 and 95 about buying and cutting plywood, and follow it carefully. Otherwise you'll not only give yourself problems and splinters, but also spoil your hard work with 'spilches' and 'gribbly holes'.

Structure

The castle is made up of two front towers with a drawbridge in between, two side walls, a look-out tower, a lock-up tower and a rear wall (see plan view, page 63). The tower walls are held together by battens of wood in the corners providing a firm substance to screw into. In addition battens of wood are screwed on to corners of the towers to form channels into which the walls are slotted. This means the castle can be assembled on fairly uneven ground successfully and can be dismantled quickly.

Drawbridge

1 Start by cutting out the entire front wall which contains the drawbridge. Now mark out the door area and cut it out carefully with a jigsaw. You can insert the jigsaw blade into the plywood in two ways:
i by drilling a series of small holes along the pencil outline, inserting the blade in one and then 'joining up the dots'.
ii by what is called 'sabre sawing'. If you look at the sole of your jigsaw (see page 91), you'll see it has a curved end. Start up the jigsaw and, holding the tool very firmly with the curved end on the plywood, slowly engage the blade with the wood. The curved sole makes it possible to 'rock' the blade into the panel. Practise on some scrap pieces first. When you've acquired the knack, you'll find it a very quick and successful method.

2 Screw a batten of wood across the bottom of the outside of the wall and another on the bottom of the outside of the door. Use four back flap hinges (available from ironmongers and DIY stores) to attach the door to the wall by screwing them into these battens of wood.

3 You will need to strengthen the door so that when it is lowered it can be walked on by parties of brave knights. Glue and screw battens to the door in the positions shown on the plan (see page 61).

4 Now for the drawbridge mechanism which is very simple. Cut slots in the wall to take the drawbridge 'chains' (rope). These need to be wide enough to ensure the rope won't rub against the plywood and fray. Drill holes in the two horizontal battens screwed on to the top of the door which stick out slightly. Knot a length of rope in each hole and thread the other ends through the slots.

5 Make the winding mechanism by first cutting a length of thick dowelling rod (or broom handle) to size. Cut out two discs of plywood and drill a hole through the middle of each to the same diameter as the rod. Then cut out two large bearing blocks which will hold the rod to the wall and drill these with the same size holes.

Glue and screw the bearing blocks to the inner face of the wall and thread the dowelling through the holes. (You'll find this easier if you rub candle wax in them first.) Push a plywood disc on to each end of the rod so that they butt up against the bearing blocks. Glue these discs firmly in position on the rod.

Mark the rod exactly in line with the slots in the wall and drill holes at these points through the rod to take the ropes. Knot the ropes into these holes with the drawbridge in the 'down' position.

6 Make the winder handle by cutting out a small block of wood and drilling a hole through the centre large enough to push it on to the end of the main dowelling rod. Drill four more holes, one in each side, and glue a length of rod in each to form 'spokes'. Glue the block onto the end of the main dowelling rod. This winder mechanism works just like a wheel brace. When you turn the spoked handle the ropes wind round the rod and the drawbridge is raised. However, when you let go, the winder handle spins round at alarming speed and the spokes could hurt a child. So, to prevent injuries, skewer a hole in four tennis balls and push one firmly onto each spoke.

7 The drawbridge is fixed in the closed position by attaching a piece of strong cord to the wall and tying a loop in the other end. Screw a cup hook into the drawbridge and loop the cord over this.

Towers

1 The two front towers are identical. Start by cutting out the three walls needed for each. Cut arrow slots in the walls as detailed in the plans and as described below. Screw a batten of wood down each side of the inner face of the front (longest) wall and then attach the side walls to the front by screwing them onto these battens. Finally, screw two battens onto the free ends of each side wall as shown on the plans (page 61). These will provide a channel into which the drawbridge wall and side walls can be slotted.

2 Now make the look-out tower, which requires three full-size walls, a shorter inner wall and a floor

i Cut out the required pieces of plywood and cut the arrow slots (see below). Screw battens in place down each side of the front and back walls (inside faces). These will project at the top to take the roof.

ii Now screw horizontal battens across the middle of the three main walls and across the top of the short inner wall, these will bear the floor. Note that you have to cut notches out of the four corners of the floor so that it fits in place around the vertical battens. Screw the side walls to the vertical battens and push the floor into position.

iii Screw more vertical battens in place as shown on the plans (page 59) to provide channels in which to slot the side and rear castle walls.

iv Finally, make the look-out tower roof and screw it to the top of the inner vertical battens.

3 The lock-up tower is misnamed really since it provides a hiding place rather than a dungeon as the door can only be locked from the inside. Otherwise little brothers might find themselves in there for weeks if big sisters 'unwittingly' forgot about them!

i Cut out the four walls and the arrow slots. Mark out the door on one of the inner walls and cut it out with a jigsaw using the same procedure as for the drawbridge.

ii Use back flap hinges to fix the door to the wall, but you will need to glue battens of timber in place on the door and wall to fix them onto since plywood is not thick enough to hold the necessary screws.

iii Cut out the latch. Cut out a piece of timber and cut a notch in it. Screw this on to the inside face of the wall for the latch to hook into. Screw the latch on to the inside of the door with a washer on

either side of the latch so that it can easily be raised and lowered.

iv Finally, fit a door stop of timber on the outside face of the door to prevent the hinges being strained if children try to push the door in. (As if the little dears would do such a thing!)

v Fix the tower walls together with vertical battens as with the other towers, and screw channels of battens in place for the rear and side castle walls to slot into.

Cutting the arrow slots

The arrow slots in the tower walls and main walls need careful working.

1 Firstly mark out the shape of the slot on the plywood. If you have two or more duplicate walls (e.g. the two front walls of the front towers) it saves time if you cut the slots for all of them in one operation.

2 Hold down the sheets, one on top of the other, very firmly. Place a scrap piece of board underneath the sheets to reduce the number of splinters when the drill or jigsaw breaks through. You could also tape over the area you are working on as an extra precaution.

3 Using a flat bit, drill the holes at the four ends of the arrow slot cross. Insert the jigsaw blade in a hole and cut out the slots.

4 Glasspaper smooth the edges of the cut plywood.

Assembly

1 Cut out the two side walls and the rear wall of the castle.

2 Slot the rear wall into place between the look-out and lock-up tower.

3 Slot the side walls in place between the look-out and lock-up towers and the front towers.

4 Slot the drawbridge wall in place between the two front towers.

As you will see, this push-fit method of construction means you can compensate for slightly uneven ground, though you should not attempt to erect the castle on anything steeper than a very gradual slope.

If you find the structure isn't rigid enough you could bore holes in the vertical battens and push dowel rods through for extra strength. However, the ten children who played in the prototype for the photograph on pages 56–7 found no problems with its stability.

Finishing

Do go over the entire castle diligently with glasspaper, removing splinters and rounding off corners. Painting the castle is

fun and will give your artistic tendencies great scope, but make sure you use an exterior grade paint (see page 95). I painted black lines to simulate stone work and outlined the arrow slots in red. You could paint grass and flowers around the base of the walls for a romantic castle. I also painted the look-out tower roof and the drawbridge winder handle red and my son made a St George's flag from cardboard which we attached to the walls with a dowel rod and tape.

Bows, arrows, swords and shields

1 The bows are made by planing down batten until it is sufficiently thin to be bent. Drill holes in either end and thread a piece of nylon cord through the holes. Bind the middle of the bow with plastic insulation tape. The tape makes a good centre marker for children to place the arrow on and also helps to prevent the bow splitting in the middle.

It is a good idea with a bow to flex it several times before attempting to use it – a case of training the wood to bend!

2 The arrows are made from standard dowel rod with a slot cut in the end to fit the string. The dowel rod *must* be fitted with a lump of Blu-tack or a rubber sucker. Do impress on your children that they should aim at 'things' and *not* people. Although they are only toys they are quite capable of inflicting serious damage to eyes if not used sensibly.

3 The short swords are made from batten with a small hand guard fitted at the handle end. The hand guard has a trench cut in it that corresponds to the width of the blade. The hand guard is glued and screwed in place. *Do* make sure that all edges are rounded and, once again, that the children are taught how to use the swords sensibly.

4 The shields are the same as for the Viking boat (see page 31).

Children need time to play – to explore the world around them and use their imaginations. But they do need to be taught that there are some things that are dangerous and that their friends can get hurt unless they are careful.

I feel very strongly that children should be able to play in castles, use swords, bows and arrows, play hide and seek, climb trees, ride bicycles and so on. But our part as adults is to give them some understanding of the dangers involved and how to avoid them. This castle has given ten of my friends a wonderful afternoon of fun. I do hope it will give you and your children equal pleasure.

Cutting list

Side and rear walls	3 off	1220 × 1220 × 9mm (48 × 48 × ⅜in)	Plywood
Front wall	1 off	1524 × 1220 × 9mm (60 × 48 × ⅜in)	Plywood
	1 off	1220 × 102 × 22mm (48 × 4 × ⅞in)	Timber
	2 off	137 × 95 × 44mm (5⅜ × 3¾ × 1¾in)	Timber
Drawbridge raising bar assembly	1 off	1220mm (48in) × 22mm (⅞in) diam dowelling	
	1 off	102 × 64 × 44mm (4 × 2½ × 1¾in)	Timber
	4 off	203mm (8in) × 12mm (½in) diam dowelling	
	4 off	25mm (1in) diam spherical balls	
	2 off	89mm (3½in) diam × 9mm (⅜in) plywood discs	
Sword	as required	610 × 44 × 20mm (24 × 1¾ × ¾in)	Timber
	as required	178 × 44 × 20mm (7 × 1¾ × ¾in)	Timber
Bow	as required	1575 × 22 × 9mm (62 × ⅞ × ⅜in)	Timber
Arrow	as required	521mm (20½in) × 12mm (½in) diam dowelling	
Drawbridge assembly	1 off	1118 × 762 × 9mm (44 × 30 × ⅜in)	Plywood
	2 off	762 × 102 × 22mm (30 × 4 × ⅞in)	Timber
	2 off	984 × 89 × 22mm (38¾ × 3½ × ⅞in)	Timber
	2 off	613 × 89 × 22mm (24⅛ × 3½ × ⅞in)	Timber
	2 off	295 × 47 × 22mm (11⅝ × 1⅞ × ⅞in)	Timber
Front tower – right and left hand	2 off	1220 × 610 × 9mm (48 × 24 × ⅜in)	Plywood
	4 off	1220 × 305 × 9mm (48 × 12 × ⅜in)	Plywood
	4 off	1220 × 47 × 22mm (48 × 1⅞ × ⅞in)	Timber
	4 off	1118 × 47 × 22mm (44 × 1⅞ × ⅞in)	Timber
	4 off	1220 × 98 × 22mm (48 × 3⅞ × ⅞in)	Timber
Lock-up tower	4 off	1220 × 610 × 9mm (48 × 24 × ⅜in)	Plywood
	6 off	1220 × 47 × 22mm (48 × 1⅞ × ⅞in)	Timber
	2 off	1220 × 98 × 22mm (48 × 3⅞ × ⅞in)	Timber
	1 off	660 × 47 × 22mm (26 × 1⅞ × ⅞in)	Timber
Door	1 off	813 × 305 × 9mm (32 × 12 × ⅜in)	Plywood
	1 off	660 × 47 × 22mm (26 × 1⅞ × ⅞in)	Timber
	1 off	121 × 28 × 22mm (4¾ × 1⅛ × ⅞in)	Timber
	2 off	127 × 44 × 22mm (5 × 1¾ × ⅞in)	Timber
Latch	1 off	70 × 64 × 22mm (6¾ × 2½ × ⅞in)	Timber
Look-out tower	3 off	1220 × 610 × 9mm (48 × 24 × ⅜in)	Plywood
	1 off	610 × 508 × 9mm (24 × 20 × ⅜in)	Plywood
	1 off	610 × 590 × 9mm (24 × 23¼ × ⅜in)	Plywood
	4 off	1829 × 47 × 22mm (72 × 1⅞ × ⅞in)	Timber
	2 off	1220 × 47 × 22mm (48 × 1⅞ × ⅞in)	Timber
	2 off	1220 × 98 × 22mm (48 × 3⅞ × ⅞in)	Timber
	2 off	514 × 47 × 22mm (20¼ × 1⅞ × ⅞)	Timber
	2 off	546 × 47 × 22mm (21½ × 1⅞ × ⅞in)	Timber
Look-out tower roof frame	4 off	432 × 86 × 22mm (17 × 3⅜ × ⅞in)	Timber
	2 off	102 × 60 × 22mm (4 × 2⅜ × ⅞in)	Timber
Look-out tower roof panel	2 off	838 × 457 × 9mm (33 × 18 × ⅜in)	Plywood
Flag pole	1 off	1829mm (72in) × 12mm (½in) diam dowelling	
Flag	1 off	483 × 381 × 6mm (19 × 15 × ¼in)	Plywood

Ancillaries

	4 off	102mm (4in) long × 38mm (1½in) wide hinges
	2 off	32mm (1¼in) long × 38mm (1½in) wide hinges
	1 off	3.65 metres (12ft) strong cord

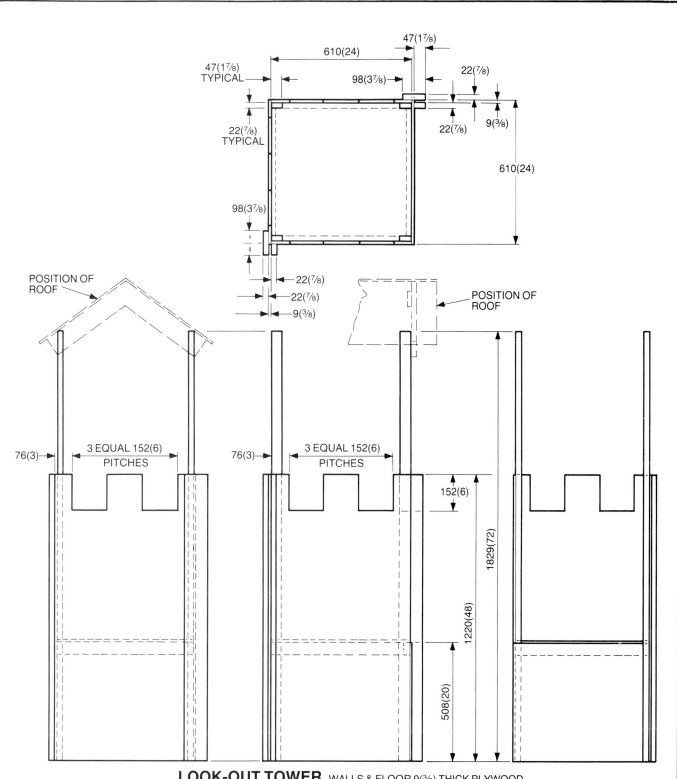

47(1⅞)
TYPICAL

22(⅞)
TYPICAL

98(3⅞)

610(24)

98(3⅞)

47(1⅞)

22(⅞)

22(⅞)

9(⅜)

610(24)

22(⅞)

22(⅞)

9(⅜)

POSITION OF ROOF

POSITION OF ROOF

76(3)

3 EQUAL 152(6)
PITCHES

76(3)

3 EQUAL 152(6)
PITCHES

152(6)

1829(72)

1220(48)

508(20)

LOOK-OUT TOWER WALLS & FLOOR 9(⅜) THICK PLYWOOD

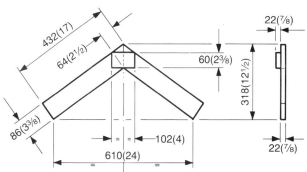

432(17)

64(2½)

60(2⅜)

318(12½)

22(⅞)

86(3⅜)

102(4)

610(24)

22(⅞)

LOOK-OUT TOWER ROOF FRAME
MAKE TWO

LOOK-OUT TOWER ROOF PANEL
838 × 457 × 9(33 × 18 × ⅜) THICK PLYWOOD
MAKE TWO

FLAG POLE
1829 × 12(72 × ½) DIAM DOWEL

FLAG
483 × 381 × 6(19 × 15 × ¼) PLYWOOD
70(2¾)WIDE RED BARS PAINTED
ON WHITE BACKGROUND

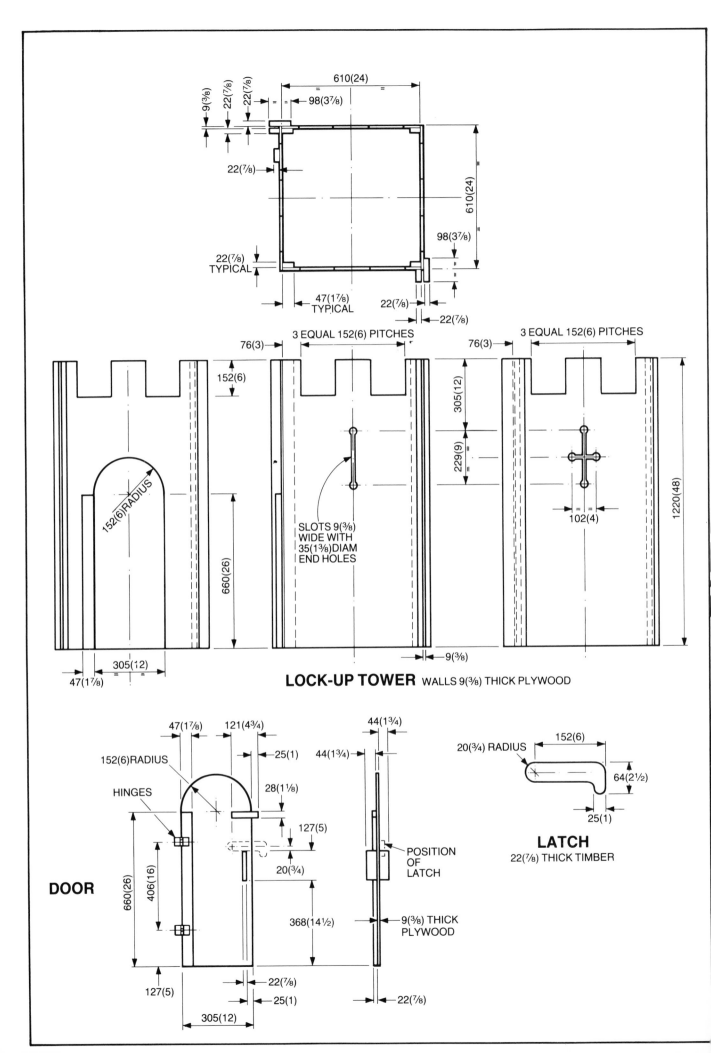

610(24)

98(3⅞)

9(⅜)
22(⅞)
22(⅞)

22(⅞)

610(24)

98(3⅞)

22(⅞)
TYPICAL

47(1⅞)
TYPICAL

22(⅞)

22(⅞)

76(3)   3 EQUAL 152(6) PITCHES   76(3)   3 EQUAL 152(6) PITCHES

152(6)

305(12)

229(9)

152(6)RADIUS

660(26)

1220(48)

SLOTS 9(⅜)
WIDE WITH
35(1⅜)DIAM
END HOLES

102(4)

305(12)

47(1⅞)

9(⅜)

LOCK-UP TOWER WALLS 9(⅜) THICK PLYWOOD

47(1⅞)   121(4¾)

44(1¾)

44(1¾)

152(6)RADIUS

25(1)

20(¾) RADIUS

152(6)

HINGES

28(1⅛)

127(5)

64(2½)

406(16)

660(26)

POSITION
OF
LATCH

25(1)

20(¾)

LATCH
22(⅞) THICK TIMBER

368(14½)

DOOR

9(⅜) THICK
PLYWOOD

127(5)

22(⅞)

25(1)

22(⅞)

305(12)

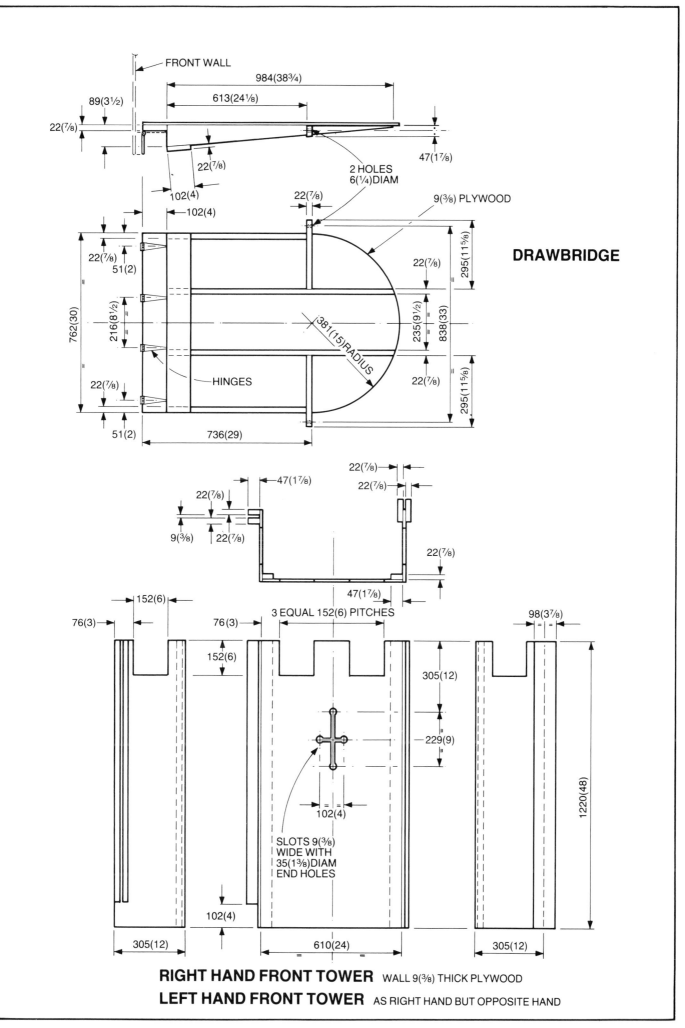

FRONT WALL

984(38¾)

613(24⅛)

89(3½)

22(⅞)

102(4)

22(⅞)

102(4)

22(⅞)

47(1⅞)

2 HOLES
6(¼)DIAM

22(⅞)

9(⅜) PLYWOOD

DRAWBRIDGE

22(⅞)
51(2)

22(⅞)

295(11⅝)

762(30)

216(8½)

381(15)RADIUS

235(9½)

838(33)

HINGES

22(⅞)

22(⅞)
51(2)

22(⅞)

295(11⅝)

736(29)

22(⅞)

47(1⅞)

22(⅞)

22(⅞)

9(⅜)

22(⅞)

22(⅞)

47(1⅞)

152(6)

3 EQUAL 152(6) PITCHES

98(3⅞)

76(3)

76(3)

152(6)

152(6)

305(12)

229(9)

102(4)

1220(48)

SLOTS 9(⅜)
WIDE WITH
35(1⅜)DIAM
END HOLES

305(12)

102(4)

305(12)

610(24)

RIGHT HAND FRONT TOWER WALL 9(⅜) THICK PLYWOOD

LEFT HAND FRONT TOWER AS RIGHT HAND BUT OPPOSITE HAND

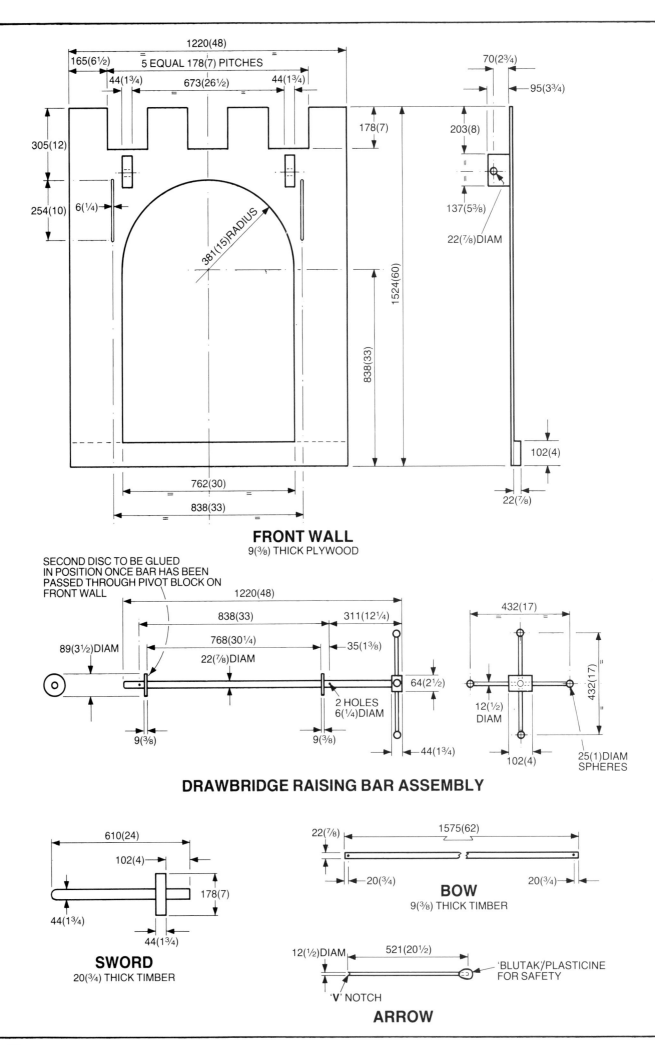

FRONT WALL
9(³⁄₈) THICK PLYWOOD

1220(48)
165(6½)
5 EQUAL 178(7) PITCHES
44(1¾)
673(26½)
44(1¾)
178(7)
305(12)
254(10)
6(¼)
381(15)RADIUS
1524(60)
838(33)
762(30)
838(33)
70(2¾)
95(3¾)
203(8)
137(5⅜)
22(⅞)DIAM
102(4)
22(⅞)

SECOND DISC TO BE GLUED
IN POSITION ONCE BAR HAS BEEN
PASSED THROUGH PIVOT BLOCK ON
FRONT WALL

1220(48)
838(33)
311(12¼)
768(30¼)
35(1⅜)
89(3½)DIAM
22(⅞)DIAM
64(2½)
2 HOLES
6(¼)DIAM
9(⅜)
9(⅜)
44(1¾)
432(17)
432(17)
12(½)
DIAM
102(4)
25(1)DIAM
SPHERES

DRAWBRIDGE RAISING BAR ASSEMBLY

610(24)
102(4)
178(7)
44(1¾)
44(1¾)

SWORD
20(¾) THICK TIMBER

22(⅞)
1575(62)
20(¾)
20(¾)

BOW
9(⅜) THICK TIMBER

12(½)DIAM
521(20½)
'BLUTAK'/PLASTICINE
FOR SAFETY
'V' NOTCH

ARROW

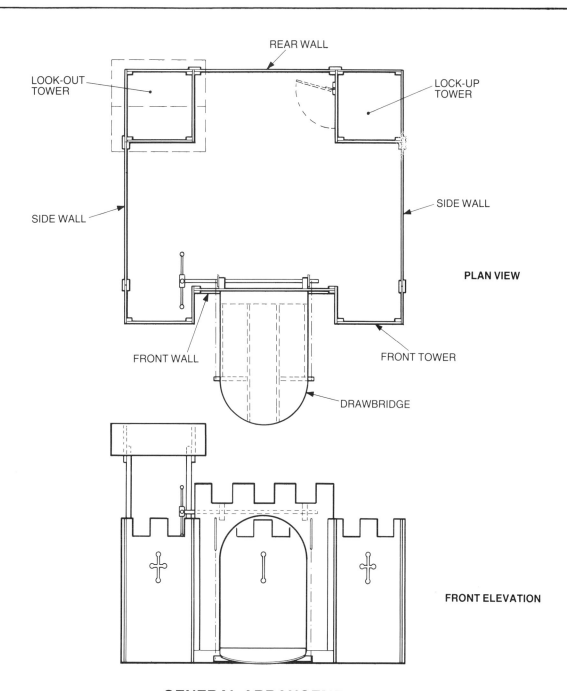

LOOK-OUT
TOWER

REAR WALL

LOCK-UP
TOWER

SIDE WALL

SIDE WALL

PLAN VIEW

FRONT WALL

FRONT TOWER

DRAWBRIDGE

FRONT ELEVATION

GENERAL ARRANGEMENT

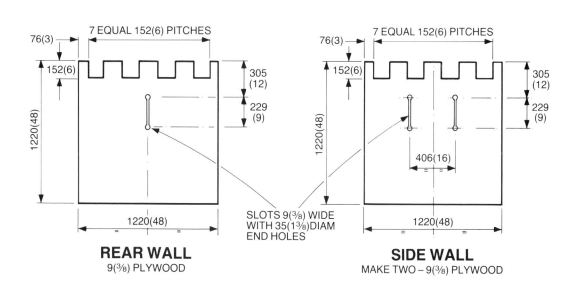

76(3)

7 EQUAL 152(6) PITCHES

152(6)

305
(12)

229
(9)

1220(48)

1220(48)

SLOTS 9(³/₈) WIDE
WITH 35(1³/₈)DIAM
END HOLES

REAR WALL
9(³/₈) PLYWOOD

76(3)

7 EQUAL 152(6) PITCHES

152(6)

305
(12)

229
(9)

1220(48)

406(16)

1220(48)

SIDE WALL
MAKE TWO – 9(³/₈) PLYWOOD

Fire engine

TROJAN HORSE

Children love things they can climb on to and if you can get inside and hide – well, that's a real bonus! So the legend of this famous horse and the part it played in the downfall of Troy inspired me to make the ultimate hide-and-seek toy.

The timber I used was Nordic redwood, which you can buy easily in a ready-planed state, or you can save a great deal of money by just getting the timber sawn and planing it yourself. However, if you decide to do this you will find the assistance of an electric planer a great boon (see page 94).

The horse is constructed entirely from pieces of timber held together with screws – there are no traditional joints. The screws I used are the new pattern 'superscrew', but, whatever you use, be sure to buy zinc-plated screws or ones especially designed for out of doors, as ordinary steel screws will rust over a very short period of time and leave nasty rust stains on the wood.

I Start by making the two ends of the horse (i.e. the front and rear walls). Cramp together the three planks for each end, then screw the cross-piece across each to hold them together. Bear in mind when positioning these cross-pieces that you are going to have to cut a curve around the top of each end for the horse's 'back'. They should be screwed in place just below where the curve starts.

2 To draw the curve, tie a marking pencil on to a piece of string. Hold the other end of the string on the central point (marked on the plans) making sure that the length of string between nail and pencil is 250mm (10in) to give you the correct radius. Holding the string taut, sweep the pencil round in an arc to give you the required curve. Repeat on the other end wall. Using an electric jigsaw, cut out the curve on each wall. You should also mark and cut away a section at the bottom of each side of each wall (see plans) to give the slanting-in effect for the horse's sides.

3 Now cut out the two pieces of timber that will hold the neck in place and screw them to the front wall.
Make the tail by cutting out a template (see page 90), drawing round it on a suitable piece of timber and cutting the shape out with a jigsaw. Smooth away any sharp edges with glasspaper, then screw the tail to the end wall from the inside face of the wall.

4 The front and rear walls are held together with a 'skin' of slats, which are narrower on the horse's 'back' than on its 'sides' to give a nice smooth curve.
Assemble all your slats of the different sizes, cut to length, and drill countersunk pilot holes (see page 93) for the screws that will attach them all to the walls. The screws must be countersunk to ensure children don't scratch themselves on the metal heads.
Bore 25mm (1in) peep holes (which will also provide extra ventilation) along one or two of the wider side slats. Note that two of the slats should be shorter than the others (see steps 5 and 13).
To help young children climb up, you can cut foot-holds in the side slats. The

only trouble is that you then no longer have a secret hiding place inside. It will depend on the age of your children what you decide to do about this.

5 Fixing the slats on to the ends is easier if you have a helper, but if you don't, wedge one end firmly against a wall or the workbench. Screw the slats in place on this end, starting with the one in the centre of the horse's 'back'. When all are in position, screw the other ends of the slats on to the other end wall. The two shorter slats should be screwed on last at the bottom of the horse's sides.

6 Once the barrel-shaped body is complete you'll need to do a great deal of sanding to remove all the sharp edges. If you know someone who has an electric belt sander, this will do the job very quickly. Make sure you give plenty of attention to each slat edge by using a piece of glasspaper wrapped round a thin piece of plywood. Spend plenty of time on this job, tiresome though it is.

7 Cut out the two pieces of timber for the 'rump' which will help to prevent children from falling off the horse backwards. Screw them together and then screw the assembled 'rump' to the end wall.

8 Now for the head and neck. First make the neck assembly by cutting out and shaping the neck piece (see page 69) and then drilling a hole for the dowel rod handle. Cut out the two spacer blocks for this handle and drill holes for the dowel rod in these too.
For the head you will first need to make a template (see page 90), following the shape shown on the plans. Draw round this on to your timber and cut out the shape using a jigsaw. Mark and cut out the mane, eyes and mouth from offcuts of wood, using the same method. Glasspaper all the pieces carefully.
Glue the eyes and mouth on to either side of the head. Then, attach the head to the neck by means of the mane pieces. These should be glued and screwed on to either side as shown on the plans.

9 Clamp the neck in position between the two pieces of timber that you previously screwed to the front wall. Drill two large holes for the dowel rods that then will hold the neck in place straight through all three pieces of timber in one operation. Push dowel rods, cut to the appropriate length, through the holes. If you leave these 'dry' and don't glue them in position you will be able to remove the head easily if you want to store the horse in your shed during the winter.

10   Now you should make the floor panel. This is made from three planks of wood, one of which is much shorter than the other two. In addition, the two longer pieces need to have sections cut away so that, when assembled, you have an access hole large enough for a child to climb through.

Clamp the three pieces together and glue and screw the cross member in place that will hold them together. I can imagine nothing worse than a child getting

stuck in a horse, so *please* make the hole large enough for your children!

11 Fix the floor panel in place by driving screws through the panel and into the ends of the front and rear walls and into the edges of the bottom body slats. You will have to drive them in at an angle along the sides in order to get them firmly into the wood. It is very important to use plenty of screws for this job as the floor panel has to bear the full weight of a child inside.

12 Now make the stand. First mark and cut out the eight legs, which all have angles (see page 90) cut on the tops and bottoms so that they 'splay' widely and give the horse plenty of stability. Now cut to length the six cross members for the sides. Finally cut the cross members for the ends of the stand – you need two long ones for the bottom which need angles cut on the ends, and two shorter ones for the top which should have the corners chamfered off (see page 91) for safety reasons.

13 Assembling the stand on to the horse is a little tricky. The easiest method is probably to prop the horse up on some blocks or a workmate of the same height as the stand. Screw the two shorter cross members with the chamfered ends on to the bottom of the front and rear walls of the horse. The two shorter slats at the bottom of the horse's sides provide space to accommodate these cross members. Make sure they are well screwed on as they will have to bear all the weight of children climbing on to and into the horse.

14 Now cramp all the legs in place, two for each corner, and use a long batten of wood placed across the sides of the legs to ensure they are all projecting at the right angle. When you are happy with the positioning of the legs, and are sure that all the 'feet' are flat on the floor, bore the holes for the coach bolts (see page 94) that will hold the legs to the horse (two bolts for each set of legs). Fit the bolts with the nuts on the inside face of the cross members.

15 Place the long cross members between the 'feet' of the horse (see plans), drill holes for coach bolts and then fit the bolts, again with the nuts on the inside face of the legs.

16 Screw the side cross members in place – three on each side. These provide climbing steps as well as giving rigidity to the frame.

17 All the countersunk screw holes should now be filled with a stopping such as Brummer Stopping (see page 93), and the legs, head, tail and body thoroughly glasspapered again to remove any rough edges. Special attention should be given to the coach bolts – these can give very nasty scratches, so file off cleanly where the bolt comes through the nut, and cover the nut with a piece of plastic insulation tape. See page 95 for advice on wood preservatives to protect the horse.

On my horse, I left two side planks that could easily be removed if a child got stuck. Don't fill the countersunk screw holes here and, if possible, use shorter screws. Mark this emergency exit with a dab of red paint. I have already mentioned the need to bore large spy/air holes and extra holes can be bored in the floor without spoiling the hiding place. A child could become very uncomfortable if stuck in the horse on a hot summer day – so lots of air holes please and an emergency exit.

Cutting list

Stand	2 off	1180 × 98 × 22mm (46½ × 3⅞ × ⅞in)	Timber
	2 off	775 × 98 × 22mm (30½ × 3⅞ × ⅞in)	Timber
	8 off	712 × 98 × 22mm (28 × 3⅞ × ⅞in)	Timber
	6 off	835 × 98 × 22mm (32⅞ × 3⅞ × ⅞in)	Timber
Floor	3 off	835 × 181 × 22mm (32⅞ × 7⅛ × ⅞in)	Timber
	1 off	543 × 86 × 22mm (21⅜ × 3⅜ × ⅞in)	Timber
Rump	1 off	318 × 178 × 22mm (12½ × 7 × ⅞in)	Timber
	1 off	165 × 98 × 22mm (6½ × 3⅞ × ⅞in)	Timber
Front wall	3 off	685 × 178 × 22mm (27 × 7 × ⅞in)	Timber
	2 off	330 × 98 × 22mm (13 × 3⅞ × ⅞in)	Timber
	1 off	521 × 98 × 22mm (20½ × 3⅞ × ⅞in)	Timber
Rear wall	3 off	685 × 178 × 22mm (27 × 7 × ⅞in)	Timber
	1 off	521 × 98 × 22mm (20½ × 3⅞ × ⅞in)	Timber
Body skinning	10 off	790 × 98 × 22mm (31⅛ × 3⅞ × ⅞in)	Timber
	13 off	790 × 48 × 22mm (31⅛ × 1⅞ × ⅞in)	Timber
Neck	1 off	902 × 178 × 22mm (35½ × 7 × ⅞in)	Timber
	2 off	95 × 70 × 22mm (3¾ × 2¾ × ⅞in)	Timber
	1 off	318mm (12½in) × 16mm (⅝in) diam dowelling	
	2 off	152mm (6in) × 16mm (⅝in) diam dowelling	
Tail	1 off	584 × 203 × 22mm (23 × 8 × ⅞in)	Timber
Head and mane	1 off	381 × 178 × 22mm (15 × 7 × ⅞in)	Timber
	2 off	483 × 114 × 22mm (19 × 4½ × ⅞in)	Timber
	2 off	229 × 76 × 22mm (9 × 3 × ⅞in)	Timber
	2 off	203 × 76 × 22mm (8 × 3 × ⅞in)	Timber
	2 off	102 × 51 × 12mm (4 × 2 × ½in)	Timber
Eyes and mouth	offcuts	22mm (⅞in) thick timber	

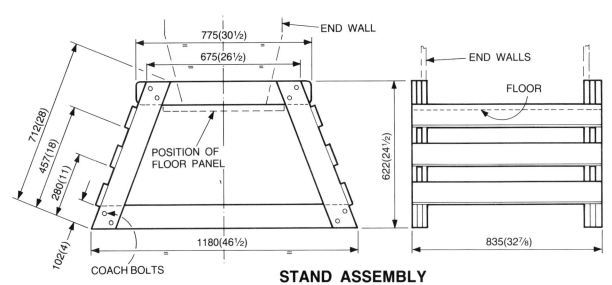

STAND ASSEMBLY
CONSTRUCTED IN 98 x 22(3⅞ x ⅞) TIMBER

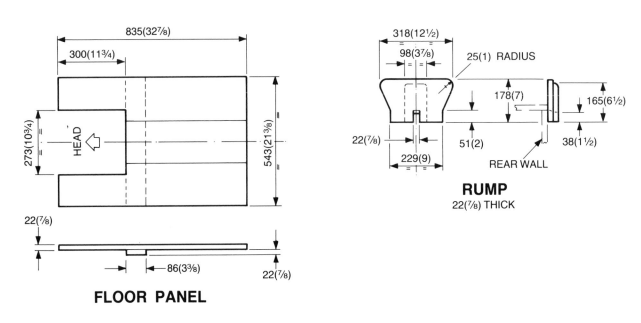

FLOOR PANEL

RUMP
22(⅞) THICK

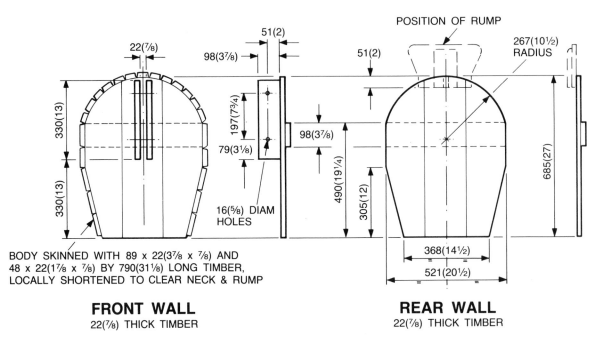

BODY SKINNED WITH 89 x 22(3⅞ x ⅞) AND
48 x 22(1⅞ x ⅞) BY 790(31⅛) LONG TIMBER,
LOCALLY SHORTENED TO CLEAR NECK & RUMP

FRONT WALL
22(⅞) THICK TIMBER

REAR WALL
22(⅞) THICK TIMBER

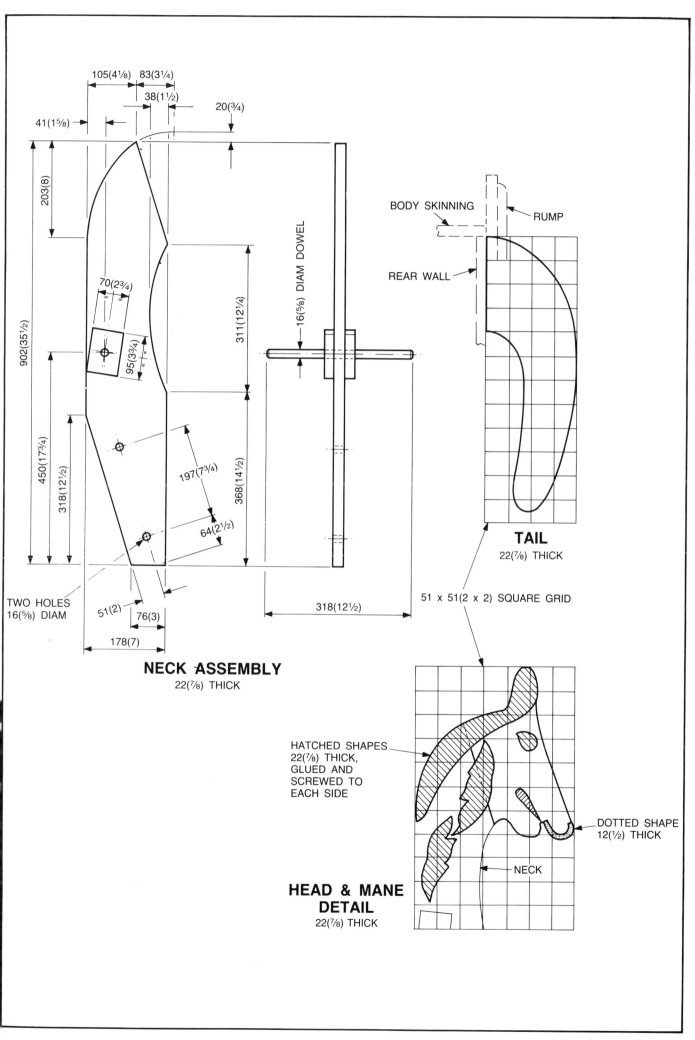

105(4⅛) 83(3¼)

38(1½)

20(¾)

41(1⅝)

203(8)

70(2¾)

95(3¾)

902(35½)

311(12¼)

16(⅝) DIAM DOWEL

450(17¾)

318(12½)

368(14½)

197(7¾)

64(2½)

TWO HOLES
16(⅝) DIAM

51(2)

76(3)

318(12½)

178(7)

NECK ASSEMBLY
22(⅞) THICK

BODY SKINNING

RUMP

REAR WALL

TAIL
22(⅞) THICK

51 x 51(2 x 2) SQUARE GRID

HATCHED SHAPES
22(⅞) THICK,
GLUED AND
SCREWED TO
EACH SIDE

DOTTED SHAPE
12(½) THICK

NECK

**HEAD & MANE
DETAIL**
22(⅞) THICK

GARDEN HOUSE

Most children have a cherished dream – a small house, shed or den which is especially for them to play in. The world of make-believe is one to foster and this little house is ideal for tea parties, teddy bears' picnics, or, stretching the imagination, a place of safety for those three little pigs who were always having trouble with the big bad wolf.

The house is built completely from stock size Nordic redwood. (I bought sawn timber and planed it up and saved a great deal of money that way.) The roof is made from corrugated 'plastic' sheeting which overlaps at the ridge and prevents the rain getting in. The design is easily adapted if you want a larger house and you can add clear plastic to the sides if you wish.

I have deliberately avoided a door. Doors need hinges and with this particular size of timber a door could give little fingers a very nasty pinch. Plywood doors are not so dangerous as they are much lighter, should you be commissioned to fit a door by the 'owner-to-be'.

The finished project always looks far more difficult than it is so let's make a start by 'breaking it down'. The house consists of two pentagonal (five-sided) frames and these are held together by lengths of wood. One of the end frames is panelled, the other left open for the entrance. The roof is held to the building by battens that are in turn fitted to the end frames.

The most important tool in this job will be a sliding bevel gauge (see page 90). If you don't have one, then get one you must, as it's vital for marking out and checking angles.

1   To make your first end frame, set the angle on the bevel gauge and mark off the required angles on the ends of the two side spars. Place the side spars and the top two spars in their correct positions on the workbench. Re-set the bevel gauge and mark off the required angles on the top spars. Place the bottom spar across and use a clamp (see page 92) to hold everything in place. When you are *sure* you have marked all the angles correctly, dismantle the frame and cut away the waste wood.

2   Screw the side spars on to the bottom spar and the top spars on to the side spars from the inside face of the frame. Where the top spars meet in the middle, screw a small shaped end plate of timber to hold them rigid.

3   Now make the other end frame in the same way. You'll find you will do this in half the time it took you to make the first one since you will have learnt so much!

4   Tape or clamp the completed end frames together and mark the notches for the top spars that will support the roof. Separate the frames and cut out the notches.

5   Cut out the eight horizontal battens needed (four for each side) that hold the end frames together. Three of these fit flat against the sides of the end frames, while the fourth fits across the ends of the bottom spars. Screw them in position by driving screws into the edges of the end frames. An assistant to support the frames as you screw would be a bonus.

6   Now cut out and screw in position the four vertical battens (two for each side) that give extra stability to the horizontal spars.

7   To complete the entrance end frame cut out two horizontal and two vertical battens of timber. Set your sliding bevel gauge to the angle of the side walls. Mark off this angle on one end of each horizontal batten. Cut away the waste wood. Screw a horizontal and a vertical batten together at right angles and mark a curve on the wood across the corner. Cut away the corner and smooth off with a spokeshave and glasspaper. Repeat with the other two battens.

Glue and screw these 'entrance rails' on to the outside face of one of the end frames.

8   The panelled end looks very homely and is very satisfying to build. By using tongue and groove boards it is simple to fit the pieces together once they are cut.
i   First cut two horizontal battens to length and screw them in position.
ii   Fit the straight strips of panelling needed below the window area, using brass panel pins to attach them to the horizontal battens. The neatest way to attach the panelling is to drive panel pins through the tongues. The groove then fits over the tongue and completely hides the panel pins. There is a real sense of achievement in this job. You will also need to cut two triangular pieces for the sides.
iii   The area above the window is more tricky. You will need to use both a sliding bevel gauge and probably also cardboard templates to mark out the angled panelling required. Take your time over the marking out and you will be less likely to waste wood. The pieces should be panel-pinned to the top horizontal batten and the roof spars.

9   Cut six roof support battens to length and screw them in position in the notches cut at the top of the end frames.

10   Now for the roof. I used standard ICI Novolux corrugated sheeting for the roof. Two 6-foot (1.35 metre) sheets gave me two pieces of the right size for each half (see page 94 for advice on cutting perspex).

The sheeting for one half of the roof should extend about 20mm (¾in) beyond the ridge. The sheeting for the other half then tucks underneath, forming a waterproof join without the need for tape or sealant.

Attach the sheeting to the roof battens using the special screws and cups recommended on page 94.

11   To make sure that the perspex roof does not pose a hazard to children, the edges of the roof need to be guarded. Screw two wooden 'barge boards' on to the top of each end frame. You'll need to cut an angle on the abutting ends of each pair so that they form a good join. Then fix a wooden batten along each side of

the roof by screwing into the ends of the battens from the outside faces of the barge boards.

If the roof perspex still overlaps anywhere cut it off with a fine-toothed saw.

To add a finishing touch cut out two shaped end plates and screw one on to the apex of each end frame.

Bench

1 Cut out the two sides of the bench and screw the seat slats in position on top of the sides.

2 Cut out four legs and screw them in position.

3 Cut out two end pieces and screw them on to the ends of the bench sides for extra stability.

Finishing

Go over the entire house and bench very carefully with glasspaper until all saw cuts and rough edges have been completely removed. See page 95 for advice on wood preservatives and paints to protect the house from the elements.

Cutting list

Basic end frame	2 off	1143 × 95 × 22mm (45 × 3¾ × ⅞in)	Timber
	4 off	1130 × 95 × 22mm (44½ × 3¾ × ⅞in)	Timber
	4 off	857 × 95 × 22mm (33¾ × 3¾ × ⅞in)	Timber
	2 off	254 × 95 × 22mm (10 × 3¾ × ⅞in)	Timber
Entrance	2 off	438 × 95 × 22mm (17¼ × 3¾ × ⅞in)	Timber
	2 off	546 × 95 × 22mm (21½ × 3¾ × ⅞in)	Timber
End fascia	4 off	940 × 95 × 22mm (37 × 3¾ × ⅞in)	Timber
	2 off	222 × 89 × 12mm (8¾ × 3½ × ½in)	Timber
Clad end	1 off	1308 × 95 × 22mm (51½ × 3¾ × ⅞in)	Timber
	1 off	1130 × 95 × 22mm (44½ × 3¾ × ⅞in)	Timber
	1 off	940 × 95 × 22mm (37 × 3¾ × ⅞in)	Timber
	1 off	737 × 25 × 25mm (29 × 1 × 1in) segment	
	Make from	1285 × 89 × 16mm (506 × 3½ × ⅝in) shiplap cladding board	
Horizontal side strips	2 off	1207 × 95 × 22mm (47½ × 3¾ × ⅞in)	Timber
Inclined side strips	6 off	1207 × 95 × 22mm (47½ × 3¾ × ⅞in)	Timber
Vertical side strips	4 off	432 × 95 × 22mm (17 × 3¾ × ⅞in)	Timber
Roof support strips	6 off	1230 × 41 × 22mm (48⅜ × 1⅝ × ⅞in)	Timber
Bench	2 off	781 × 95 × 22mm (30¾ × 3¾ × ⅞in)	Timber
	7 off	305 × 95 × 22mm (12 × 3¾ × ⅞in)	Timber
	2 off	279 × 95 × 22mm (11 × 3¾ × ⅞in)	Timber
	4 off	308 × 95 × 22mm (12⅛ × 3¾ × ⅞in)	Timber

Ancillaries

	2 off	1295mm (51in) wide × 940mm (37in) long transparent corrugated plastic panels
	36 off	Roofing nails and waterproofing spats

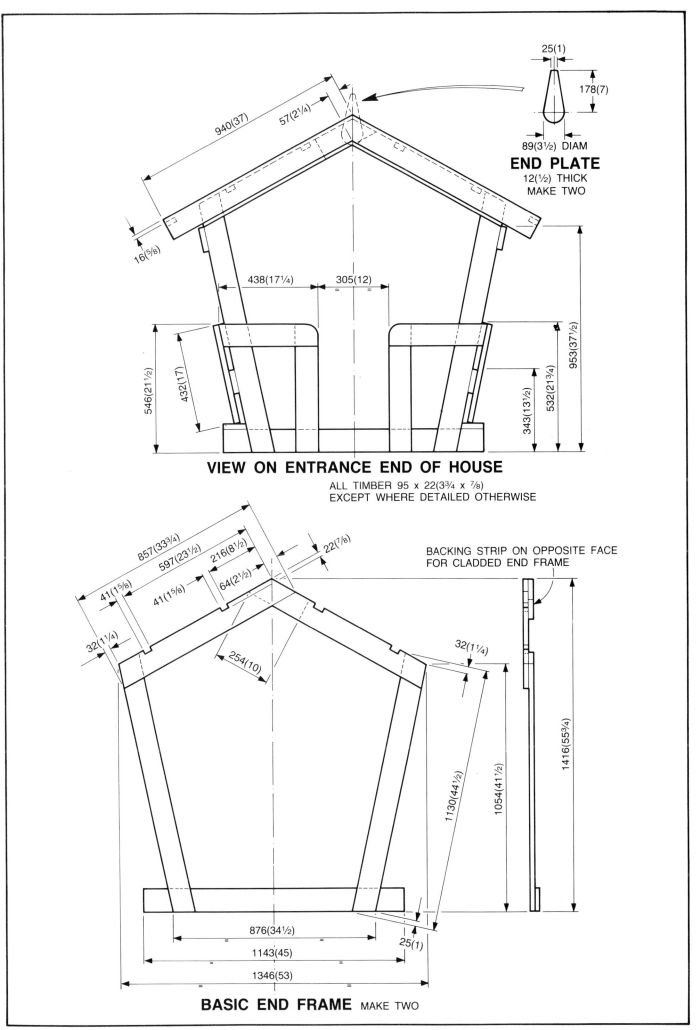

25(1)

178(7)

89(3½) DIAM

END PLATE
12(½) THICK
MAKE TWO

940(37) 57(2¼)

16(⅝)

438(17¼) 305(12)

546(21½)

432(17)

343(13½)

532(21¾)

953(37½)

VIEW ON ENTRANCE END OF HOUSE

ALL TIMBER 95 x 22(3¾ x ⅞)
EXCEPT WHERE DETAILED OTHERWISE

857(33¾)

597(23½)

216(8½)

41(1⅝)

41(1⅝)

64(2½)

22(⅞)

BACKING STRIP ON OPPOSITE FACE
FOR CLADDED END FRAME

32(1¼)

254(10)

32(1¼)

1130(44½)

1054(41½)

1416(55¾)

876(34½)

1143(45)

25(1)

1346(53)

BASIC END FRAME MAKE TWO

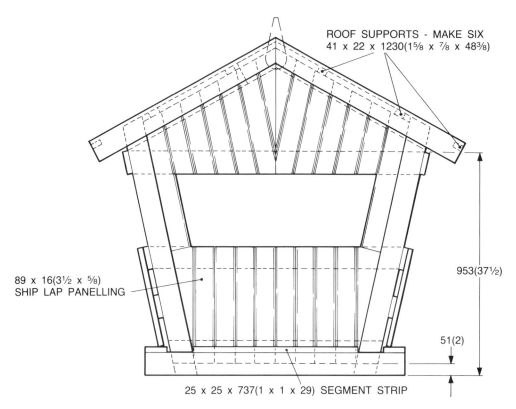

ROOF SUPPORTS - MAKE SIX
41 x 22 x 1230(1⅝ x ⅞ x 48⅜)

89 x 16(3½ x ⅝)
SHIP LAP PANELLING

953(37½)

51(2)

25 x 25 x 737(1 x 1 x 29) SEGMENT STRIP

VIEW ON CLAD END OF HOUSE

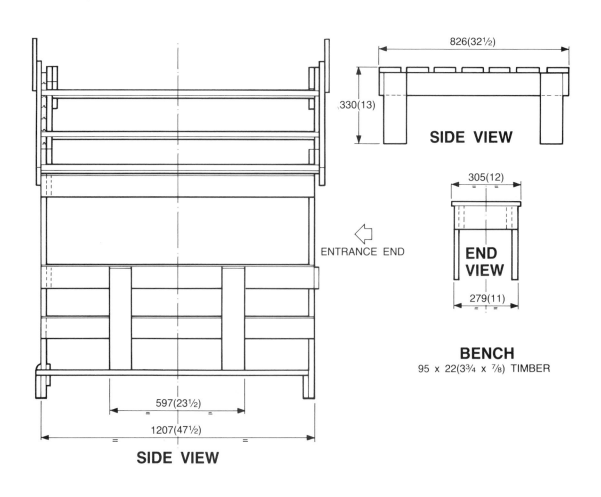

826(32½)

330(13)

SIDE VIEW

ENTRANCE END

305(12)

END VIEW

279(11)

BENCH
95 x 22(3¾ x ⅞) TIMBER

597(23½)

1207(47½)

SIDE VIEW

FIRE ENGINE

There can be few people who do not stop and look at a fire engine as it passes by. Who can ignore the urgent siren, flashing blue lights and highly polished red machine hurrying along the road to give assistance to someone somewhere? I find it most reassuring that throughout the country there are men, and now women too, willing and able to undertake dangerous rescue tasks for the general public. This fire engine is dedicated to all those who work in the fire and rescue services.

The toy is built from Nordic redwood and has a working steering wheel, spot light, bell, cable reels and a working water pump. (Well, it wouldn't be much fun playing with a fire engine if you couldn't get wet!) The bonnet slides open to show off its V6 engine complete with ignition leads, distributor and fan. The twin ladders are capable of taking the weight of an adult, so these are really useful.

The engine is designed to carry a driver and one crew member, although I am sure that extra crew could be accommodated on the rear mudguards. At first sight there appears to be a great deal to make, but there are really no difficult joints to cut and although it could not be recommended as a first woodworking project, it is easier than it looks.

1 The main chassis members are the first items to get underway. You will have to select two wide boards from the stocks of your local builder's merchant, and although these are very wide I am assured that this is a stock size width. Cut them to length, tape them together, and mark out the pieces of wood to be removed. The two cut-away areas will accommodate the front axle steering mechanism and the front bumper bar. Drill holes for the rear axles.

2 The steering mechanism is not difficult to make – providing you study the drawings carefully!

i First cut out the steering cross bar and drill the holes for the bolts that will hold the steering blocks.

ii Now cut out and shape the steering tie bar. Again, drill holes for the bolts that will attach it to the steering blocks and also a slot to accommodate the end of the steering wheel shaft.

iii Finally cut out the steering blocks themselves and drill holes for the bolts and also for the steel axles that will hold the wheels in place. Note that one of the holes for the bolts must be recessed so that the bolt head sits below the surface of the wood. Use a large flat bit to do this. Remember, too, that the holes must all be drilled at 90° in each plane (see page 93).

iv Assemble the steering mechanism by threading coach bolts (see page 94) through the cross bar, tie bar and steering blocks. I used two nuts to secure the bolts as one might come undone. Don't do these up too tightly – you need to allow for the movement of the mechanism – but when you are happy with the fit thread one nut against the other which effectively locks them in place. You'll need to apply a liberal smearing of candle grease between the wooden parts so that they move smoothly against each other.

v When you are satisfied with the steering mechanism, you can screw it to the main chassis planks by passing screws through from under the cross bar into the edges of the planks. You will first have to remove the coach bolts that hold the steering blocks to the bar. When screwed in position, re-insert the bolts, tighten up the nuts as required again and lock the two nuts in position on the end

of the bolt by tightening one against the other. (Engineers call this operation 'lock nuts'.)

3 The steering wheel shaft is a piece of mild (i.e. soft) steel rod. You need to bend this in two places to form 90° angles (see page 81) and for this you'll need a stout vice, firmly attached to a workbench, and some brute strength!

Once you have bent the shaft, you'll need to cut two small blocks of wood and drill holes to take sleeve bearings in a tight push fit. Once pushed into the holes, these bronze bearings will provide a smooth channel for the steering wheel shaft to turn in. The bearing blocks have to be screwed on to the right-hand chassis member.

At the bottom of the shaft a piece of plastic pipe over the end acts as a bearing in the slot you previously cut in the steering tie bar. When the steering wheel is turned, the shaft then activates the steering mechanism.

4 The steering wheel is an ordinary plastic wheel with some of the spokes removed. To attach it to the shaft you need to do a bit of soldering. Take a mild steel bar and drill three holes through it, using a suitable bit. Two of these will take coach bolts. The centre one, however, accommodates the steering wheel shaft, which has to be soldered in position. Ordinary soft solder will do but if you can find a local engineer who will silver solder the two pieces of steel together you will have a much stronger joint.

Now cut out the plywood steering wheel hub with a jigsaw, and drill the two holes required. To attach the steering wheel to the shaft, pass two coach bolts up through the steel bar, then between the spokes of the wheel and finally through the holes in the plywood hub. Thread nuts onto the end of each bolt and tighten them up so that the wheel is clamped on to the bar. Glue spring caps (see page 94) over the ends of the bolts (sawn off, if necessary) and over the end of the steering wheel shaft.

5 Cut out three of the four bulkheads needed to fix the two main chassis members together: the back of the engine compartment (front bulkhead), the driver's seat back and the rear bulkhead. These all need to be recessed

at the sides so that they fit snugly between the chassis members. In addition the rear bulkhead has to be drilled with three holes for the water pipes, and the seat back needs angles cut so that it can be fixed at a slight recline for driver comfort. The front bulkhead has angles cut at the top so that it will align with the engine compartment.

Glue and screw all these pieces of timber between the main chassis members, passing the screws into the edges of the bulkheads from the outside of the chassis members. Whenever a screwhead will show, counterbore the hole and plug it with wood or dowel rod (see page 93) to give a better finish. Screw two support strips of timber behind the seat back for added strength.

6 Now make the radiator. Cut out the main shape which, like the front bulkhead, has angles cut at the top so that it will align with the engine. Cut two thick and five narrower vertical battens of wood and glue them in place for the grille. A further batten across the bottom and a shaped piece across the top finish off this section. It is surprising how much character the radiator adds to the finished engine.

Glue a block of wood for the 'filler cap' on top and then screw the radiator on to the front edges of the chassis members using three long screws on each side. Again, these should be counterbored and plugged with dowel rods to hide the screw heads.

7 Cut out two discs of wood for the headlamps and drill a hole into the side of each. Glue a length of dowel rod into each hole.

8 Cut out and shape the bumper. Drill holes for the headlamps to fit into and then glue the lamps in place. Glue and screw the bumper on to the main chassis members. It fits into the recesses you cut on the front of these and you'll need long screws. They need to pass up from underneath the bumper into the edges of the chassis members.

9 Cut out the dashboard and remove the waste along one side, using a smoothing plane, to produce an angle. Cut out a slot for the steering wheel shaft. Glue and screw the dashboard on to the front bulkhead, passing the screws into it from the bonnet side of the bulkhead.

10 The windscreen is perspex and, because this has very sharp edges, I fitted a car boot seal around it. This type of rubber seal is available from the accessory and 'spare parts' departments

of most car dealers and motorists' shops. Cut out the windscreen using a metal-cutting blade in your jigsaw and screw it to the front bulkhead. The rubber seal is moulded in such a way that it simply slots on to the perspex leaving a nice rubber surround.

11 Now for the engine.
i Cut out a length of timber on which to mount the engine block and glue it in position between the two main chassis members.
ii Cut out the engine block itself and drill holes for the 'electric leads', three on each side. Drill a hole at the front for the cooling fan.
iii The cooling fan is made by cutting out a disc of plywood and then marking out 'blades' on it. The waste wood then has to be cut away with a jigsaw. Attach the fan to the front of the engine block with a long screw.
iv Finally, cut out a distributor from a piece of timber. Drill holes for the leads and a central hole. Drill a corresponding hole through the centre of a thick piece of dowelling and glue the two pieces together. Attach the distributor to the engine support member by passing a long screw through the central hole into the timber. Glue six leads (I used a co-axial cable) into the distributor and into the holes in the engine block – a V6 engine, no less!
You can detail the engine for more, if you wish.

12 For the bonnet assembly you need to cut out a short length of timber and glue and screw this between the radiator and the front bulkhead. Cutting out the bonnet flaps is a more tricky operation. These are each formed from two pieces of wood which need angles cut along both sides of the top pieces and one side of the bottom pieces. Mark the waste area to be removed carefully with pencil and, working from both ends, use a smoothing plane to achieve the required angles.

Glue the top pieces to the side pieces and when they have dried, fix them in place on to the centre of the bonnet using lengths of piano hinge.

Fit magnetic catches to keep the bonnet sides closed and cut out, shape and glue on a bonnet handle on each side.

13 Cut out the driver's seat and round off the edges with a spokeshave. Screw it in position on top of the chassis members.

14 Cut out the four chassis cross members required and screw them into position on the underside of the main

chassis members. These not only give the vehicle extra rigidity but also provide a running board and floor for the driver at the front and a support for the water container at the back.

15 Cut out the mudguards for the back wheels. These need to be glued and screwed to the chassis since children may sit or stand on them. Drive the screws into the edges of the planks from inside the chassis.

16 Cut to length a block of wood for each of the front mudguards. These involve a lot of shaping and you should read the notes on shaping tools on page 91 and make sure your tools are really sharp before you start work.

Pencil in the outline of the areas to be removed, then scribble over the waste sections to be certain you know what you are doing. Start by removing the curved wheel area with a coping saw (or bow saw if you have access to one). Then remove saw cuts with a spokeshave and glass paper. Remove the front corners with a tenon saw and smooth them into a satisfying rounded shape with a spokeshave. Finally, chamfer off the waste section at the back of each mudguard and use a firmer chisel and spokeshave to achieve a gradual slope. It is worth spending some time on these mudguards as they add tremendously to the overall effect of the fire engine.

When they are finished, glue them on to the sides of the chassis members.

17 The last stage of the main chassis is fitting the 'water tank'. The tank is simply a plastic bottle and pump-action spray such as are sold in garden centres for spraying plants with water or pesticide. You will have to do some careful measuring and then probably try several suppliers before you find the size you need. The one I used was a 2-litre spray.
i Cut out a piece of plywood to sit on top of the two cross members and provide a base for the 'tank'. Position the 'tank' on top, far forward enough so as to leave room at the back for a crew member.
ii Now make the cover for the pump compartment. Cut out a piece of plywood and mark out on it where the neck of the container has to come through. Drill a hole of the same diameter as the neck and then cut away a section of plywood from the hole out to the edge of the plywood.
iii Slot the plywood cover in position around the neck and then fit the cut-out piece back in position, glueing two small strips of wood underneath to support it.

iv Screw the cover on to the top of the main chassis members. Use cup washers under the screw heads so that you can remove the cover easily if necessary.

18 The engine completed, you can now turn your attention to the ladders. Cut four lengths of knot-free timber for the ladder sides. Tape or clamp two together and mark the position of the rungs. Using a flat bit, drill the holes for the rungs with the two lengths still fixed together. Repeat this procedure with the other two lengths. Make sure the holes are drilled at 90° in both planes (see page 93). Round off the ends of the ladder sides with a smoothing plane and spokeshave.

I used broom handles for the rungs which are cheaper than thick dowelling. Cut all the rungs for the wider ladder to length and glasspaper the ends to round them off. Apply glue to one end of each rung and fix them into the rung holes of one ladder side. Chamfer off the free ends and apply glue. Carefully line up the ends into the other ladder side and, using a block of waste wood under a hammer, gently tap the side evenly on to all the rungs. Aim to get all the rungs just started.

Now fit the ladder in your vice and tighten up along the whole length. Stop when all the ends of the rungs are flush with the outside of the ladder sides.

Repeat the procedure for the narrower ladder which differs only in that the rungs are shorter.

19 The ladders are supported by a framework of timber battens and dowel rods.

Cut the four pairs of dowel rods to length. Cut out the two horizontal battens for the rear supports and drill the holes for the dowel rods.

Cut out the front vertical batten and also the two mounting blocks that will fit on to the front mudguards. These require some shaping using a coping saw? Drill holes for the dowel rods.

20 Cut out the spotlight arm and drill holes for the ladder support and the spotlight bracket. The bracket is mild steel rod bent as shown on page 86 and soft-soldered in position. I fitted a battery-operated 'Vidor' lamp, but there are several different types available.

21 Glue and screw the front mounting blocks on to the mudguards. Glue the two longest dowel rods in position. Slide the spotlight arm on to the left-hand rod. Apply glue to the appropriate part of the rod and slide the arm down to that position. Support it, if necessary, while the glue dries. Glue the horizontal batten on to the tops of the dowels and glue a short pair of dowels into the top of this batten.

22 Now make the hose reels and spindle.

Cut out the two hose reel spindle blocks. Drill holes for the upright dowel rods and the spindle.

Cut out four discs of plywood and drill a central hole in each for the spindle. Drill a corresponding hole in each of two blow-moulded plastic wheels. Glue a disc on either side of each wheel (I used Araldite rapid glue).

The spindle is a mild steel rod bent at 90° in two places (as with the steering wheel shaft). In order for it to turn smoothly, you should fit a bronze sleeve bearing in each of the spindle blocks.

23 To assemble the rear ladder support, first glue and screw the bottom horizontal batten to the rear bulkhead and glue the longer pair of dowel rods in place.

Slide the spindle blocks down the rods and glue them in position as you did the spotlight arm. It is a good idea to thread the spindle in position while the glue dries to ensure the spindle blocks align.

Glue the top batten on to the dowel

rods and glue in the remaining shorter pair of dowel rods.

24 Remove the spindle and then reinsert it into the mounting blocks, threading the hose reels and three spacers made from plastic tubing in position as shown on page 86.

Fit another piece of plastic tube over the handle and hold it in place with a spring cap. Use a spring cap on the other end of the spindle to secure it in position.

Wind plastic tubing on to the hose reels.

25 Screw two tie strips of timber in position between the front and rear ladder pylon cross members. The wider of the two ladders fits snugly in between these and the narrower ladder slots into the wider one. However, luggage straps will be needed to hold the ladders securely to the support frame when the engine is racing off to an emergency.

Finishing
Before fitting the wheels, give the engine a good glasspapering all over and several coats of non-toxic paint or varnish, but do not leave the engine outside permanently for the reasons explained on page 95. I used spinnaker yacht varnish which gives a very high gloss that seemed appropriate for the project. A restrained use of red paint is also very effective.

I hung a brass bell on the front pylon cross member as a reminder of days when there was less traffic and screaming sirens weren't necessary. I used black insulation tape around the headlamps and on the bonnet handles for extra detail.

The last job is to fit the wheels. The wheels at the back need plastic spacers to position them the correct distance from the chassis. The steel rod axle ends have to be chamfered before the star lock washers are fitted (see page 94). I then fitted red hub caps.

Cutting list

Main chassis members	2 off	1025 × 191 × 22mm (40⅜ × 7½ × ⅞in)	Timber
Front bumper	1 off	451 × 98 × 22mm (17¾ × 3⅞ × ⅞in)	Timber
Headlamp	2 off	25mm (1in) × 79mm (3⅛in) diam	Timber
	2 off	70mm (2¾in) × 20mm (¾in) diam dowelling	
Rear bulkhead	1 off	362 × 254 × 22mm (14¼ × 10 × ⅞in)	Timber
Rear mudguard assembly	2 off	480 × 98 × 22mm (18⅞ × 3⅞ × ⅞in)	Timber
	4 off	165 × 98 × 22mm (6½ × 3⅞ × ⅞in)	Timber
Cross members	3 off	254 × 98 × 22mm (10 × 3⅞ × ⅞in)	Timber
R.B. cross member	1 off	451 × 168 × 22mm (17¾ × 6⅝ × ⅞in)	Timber
Steering cross bar	1 off	343 × 64 × 44mm (13½ × 2½ × 1¾in)	Timber
Steering tie bar	1 off	343 × 64 × 44mm (13½ × 2½ × 1¾in)	Timber
Steering block	2 off	127 × 64 × 44mm (5 × 2½ × 1¾in)	Timber
Front mudguard	2 off	343 × 83 × 76mm (13½ × 3¼ × 3in)	Timber
Radiator	1 off	327 × 254 × 22mm (12⅞ × 10 × ⅞in)	Timber
	1 off	254 × 47 × 22mm (10 × 1⅞ × ⅞in)	Timber
	2 off	279 × 22 × 22mm (11 × ⅞ × ⅞in)	Timber
	5 off	260 × 22 × 9mm (10¼ × ⅞ × ⅜in)	Timber
	1 off	210 × 22 × 20mm (8¼ × ⅞ × ¾in)	Timber
	1 off	25mm (1in) × 32mm (1¼in) diam dowelling	
Bonnet assembly	1 off	203 × 83 × 22mm (8 × 3¼ × ⅞in)	Timber
	2 off	203 × 108 × 22mm (8 × 4¼ × ⅞in)	Timber
	2 off	203 × 102 × 22mm (8 × 4 × ⅞in)	Timber
Bonnet handle	2 off	95 × 22 × 20mm (3¾ × ⅞ × ¾in)	Timber
Front bulkhead	1 off	292 × 254 × 22mm (11½ × 10 × ⅞in)	Timber
Dashboard	1 off	241 × 98 × 22mm (9½ × 3⅞ × ⅞in)	Timber
Steering column bearing blocks	2 off	64 × 51 × 51mm (2½ × 2 × 2in)	Timber
Seat back	1 off	476 × 254 × 22mm (18¾ × 10 × ⅞in)	Timber
Seat back support strip	2 off	197 × 22 × 16mm (7¾ × ⅞ × ⅝in)	Timber
Seat swab	1 off	254 × 133 × 22mm (10 × 5¼ × ⅞in)	Timber
Engine assembly	1 off	210 × 98 × 22mm (8¼ × 3⅞ × ⅞in)	Timber
	1 off	162 × 95 × 70mm (6⅜ × 3¾ × 2¾in)	Timber
Distributor	1 off	25mm (1in) × 57mm (2¼in) diam	Timber
	1 off	25mm (1in) × 25mm (1in) diam dowelling	
Cooling fan	1 off	9mm (⅜in) × 165mm (6½in) diam	Plywood
Steering wheel hub	1 off	127 × 76 × 6mm (5 × 3 × ¼in)	Plywood
Front ladder pylon mounting block	2 off	95 × 76 × 32mm (3¾ × 3 × 1¼in)	Timber
Ladder pylon cross member	3 off	445 × 60 × 32mm (17½ × 2⅜ × 1¼in)	Timber
Pylons	4 off	114mm (4½in) × 20mm (¾in) diam dowelling	
	2 off	572mm (22½in) × 20mm (¾in) diam dowelling	
	2 off	343mm (13½in) × 20mm (¾in) diam dowelling	
Tie strips	2 off	1067 × 38 × 22mm (42 × 1½ × ⅞in)	Timber
Spot lamp arm	1 off	178 × 64 × 41mm (7 × 2½ × 1⅝in)	Timber
Hose reel spindle block	2 off	98 × 98 × 32mm (3⅞ × 3⅞ × 1¼in)	Timber
Hose reel	4 off	9mm (⅜in) × 197mm (7¾in) diam	Timber
Ladders	4 off	1525 × 79 × 22mm (60 × 3⅛ × ⅞in)	Timber
	6 off	298mm (11¾in) × 22mm (⅞in) diam dowelling	
	6 off	248mm (9¾in) × 22mm (⅞in) diam dowelling	
Pump compartment cover	1 off	425 × 254 × 9mm (16¾ × 10 × ⅜in)	Plywood
	1 off	165 × 76 × 9mm (6½ × 3 × ⅜in)	Plywood
Pump compartment floor	1 off	381 × 127 × 9mm (15 × 5 × ⅜in)	Plywood

Ancillaries

6 off	197mm (7¾in) diam road wheels
2 off	121mm (4¾in) × 12mm (½in) diam steel front stub axles
2 off	451mm (17¾in) × 12mm (½in) diam steel rear axles
2 off	47mm (1⅞in) × 12mm (½in) ⁱdiam × 16mm (⅝in) ᵒdiam spacer tubes
6 off	12mm (½in) spring dome caps
2 off	114mm (4½in) × 6mm (¼in) diam coach bolts, nuts and washers
2 off	102mm (4in) × 6mm (¼in) diam coach bolts, nuts and washers
2 off	197mm (7¾in) × 16mm (⅝in) piano hinges
1 off	254mm (10in) × 216mm (8½in) × 1.5mm (1/16in) thick clear plastic
8 off	16mm (⅝in) × 12mm (½in) ᵒ/diam × 9mm (⅜in) ⁱ/diam plain phosphor bronze bearings
2 off	Magnetic cabinet catches
1 off	1 metre (39in) length of coaxial cable for dummy ignition leads
1 off	610mm (24in) × 9mm (⅜in) diam steel bar for steering column
1 off	127mm (5in) × 25mm (1in) × 6mm (¼in) steel strip
1 off	165mm (6½in) diam road wheel
3 off	12mm (½in) spring dome caps
2 off	38mm (1½in) × 6mm (¼in) diam coach bolts, nuts and washers
1 off	203mm (8in) × 9mm (⅜in) ⁱ/diam × 12mm (½in) ᵒ/diam plastic tube for various sleeves etc
1 off	610mm (24in) × 6mm (¼in) diam steel rod to form spotlamp frame
1 off	'Vidor' lamp
1 off	660mm (26in) × 9mm (⅜in) diam steel rod for hose reel spindle
2 off	9mm (⅜in) spring dome caps
2 off	143mm (5⅝in) diam road wheels
1 off	'Polyspray' model 3 – 2 litre pump and hose assembly
1 off	6 metres (20ft) × 6mm (¼in) bore plastic tubing

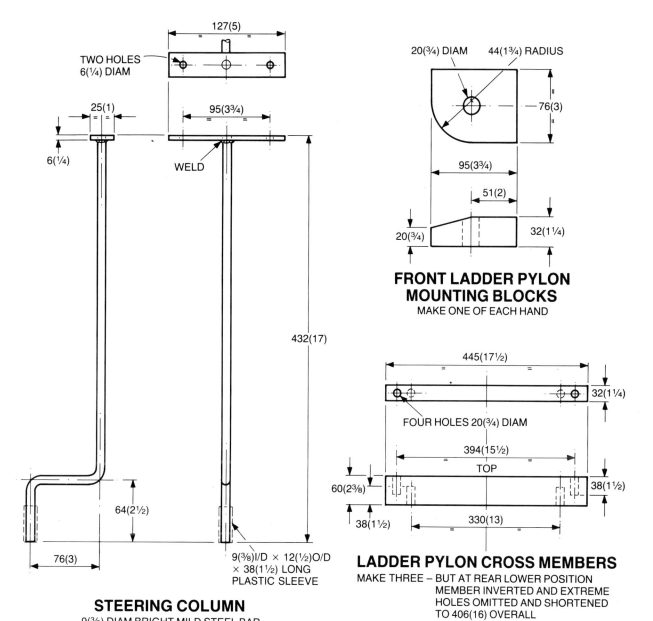

127(5)

TWO HOLES
6(¼) DIAM

25(1)

95(3¾)

6(¼)

WELD

432(17)

64(2½)

76(3)

9(⅜)I/D × 12(½)O/D
× 38(1½) LONG
PLASTIC SLEEVE

STEERING COLUMN
9(⅜) DIAM BRIGHT MILD STEEL BAR

20(¾) DIAM   44(1¾) RADIUS

76(3)

95(3¾)

51(2)

20(¾)   32(1¼)

FRONT LADDER PYLON
MOUNTING BLOCKS
MAKE ONE OF EACH HAND

445(17½)

32(1¼)

FOUR HOLES 20(¾) DIAM

394(15½)

TOP

60(2⅜)   38(1½)

38(1½)

330(13)

LADDER PYLON CROSS MEMBERS
MAKE THREE – BUT AT REAR LOWER POSITION
MEMBER INVERTED AND EXTREME
HOLES OMITTED AND SHORTENED
TO 406(16) OVERALL

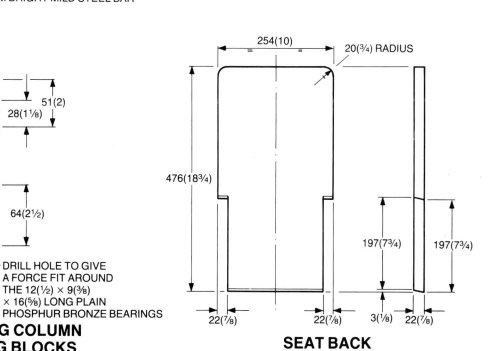

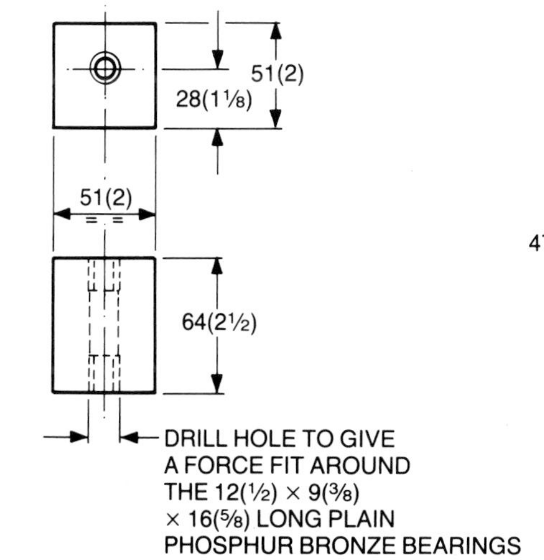

51(2)

28(1⅛)

51(2)

64(2½)

DRILL HOLE TO GIVE
A FORCE FIT AROUND
THE 12(½) × 9(⅜)
× 16(⅝) LONG PLAIN
PHOSPHUR BRONZE BEARINGS

STEERING COLUMN
BEARING BLOCKS
MAKE TWO

254(10)   20(¾) RADIUS

476(18¾)

197(7¾)   197(7¾)

22(⅞)   22(⅞)   3(⅛)   22(⅞)

SEAT BACK

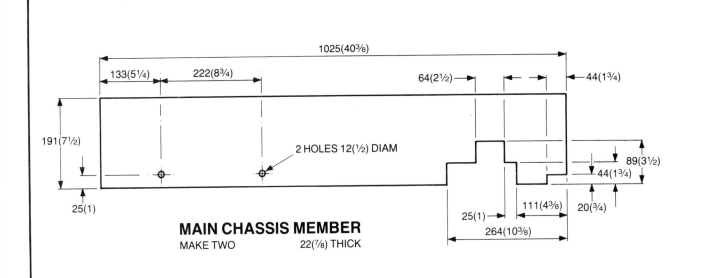

MAIN CHASSIS MEMBER
MAKE TWO   22(⅞) THICK

1025(40⅜)

133(5¼)   222(8¾)

64(2½)   44(1¾)

191(7½)

2 HOLES 12(½) DIAM

89(3½)
44(1¾)

25(1)

25(1)   111(4⅜)   20(¾)

264(10⅜)

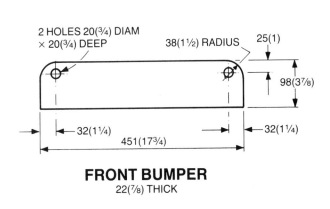

FRONT BUMPER
22(⅞) THICK

2 HOLES 20(¾) DIAM × 20(¾) DEEP

38(1½) RADIUS   25(1)

98(3⅞)

32(1¼)   451(17¾)   32(1¼)

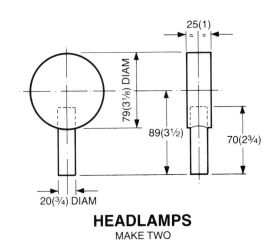

HEADLAMPS
MAKE TWO

25(1)

79(3⅛) DIAM

89(3½)

70(2¾)

20(¾) DIAM

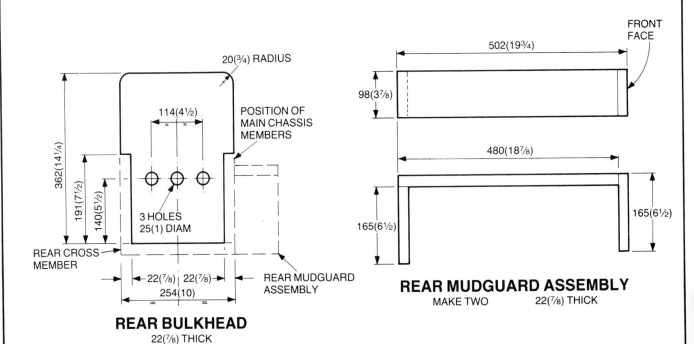

REAR BULKHEAD
22(⅞) THICK

20(¾) RADIUS

114(4½)

POSITION OF MAIN CHASSIS MEMBERS

362(14¼)
191(7½)
140(5½)

3 HOLES 25(1) DIAM

REAR CROSS MEMBER

22(⅞)   22(⅞)

254(10)

REAR MUDGUARD ASSEMBLY

REAR MUDGUARD ASSEMBLY
MAKE TWO   22(⅞) THICK

FRONT FACE

502(19¾)

98(3⅞)

480(18⅞)

165(6½)   165(6½)

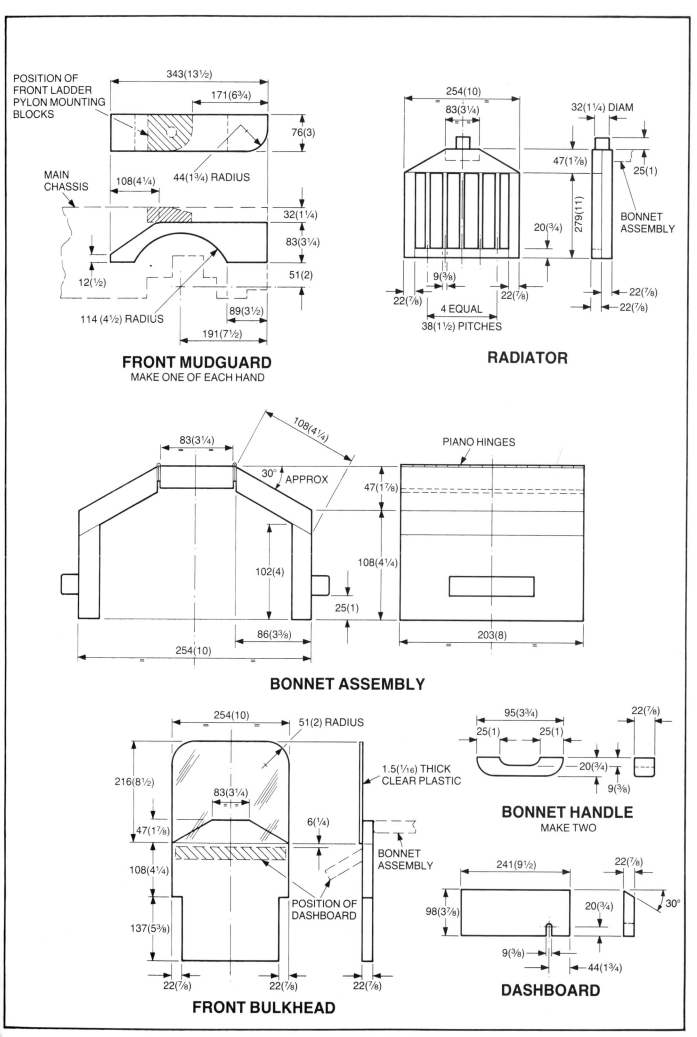

FRONT MUDGUARD
MAKE ONE OF EACH HAND

RADIATOR

BONNET ASSEMBLY

BONNET HANDLE
MAKE TWO

FRONT BULKHEAD

DASHBOARD

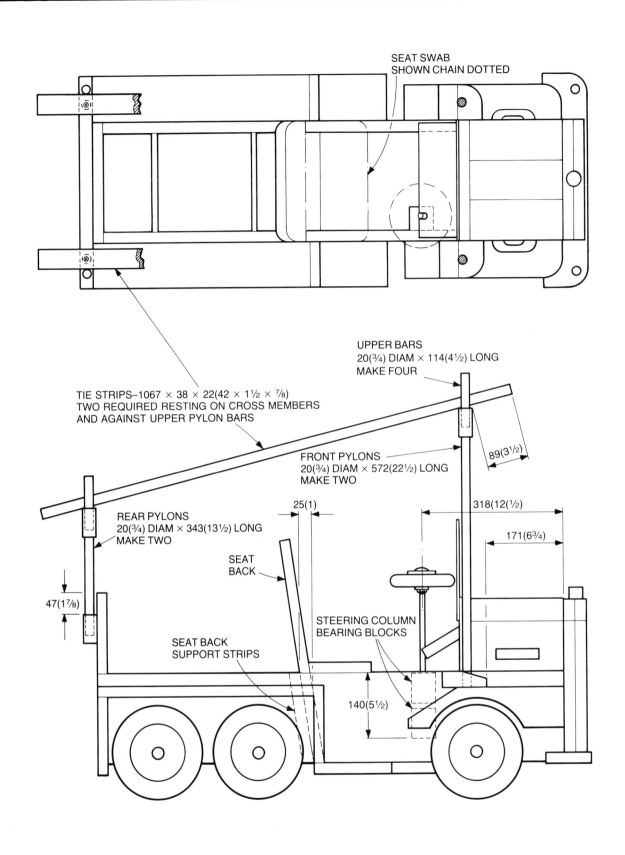

SEAT SWAB
SHOWN CHAIN DOTTED

UPPER BARS
20(¾) DIAM × 114(4½) LONG
MAKE FOUR

TIE STRIPS–1067 × 38 × 22(42 × 1½ × ⅞)
TWO REQUIRED RESTING ON CROSS MEMBERS
AND AGAINST UPPER PYLON BARS

89(3½)

FRONT PYLONS
20(¾) DIAM × 572(22½) LONG
MAKE TWO

318(12(½))

171(6¾)

REAR PYLONS
20(¾) DIAM × 343(13½) LONG
MAKE TWO

25(1)

SEAT
BACK

STEERING COLUMN
BEARING BLOCKS

47(1⅞)

SEAT BACK
SUPPORT STRIPS

140(5½)

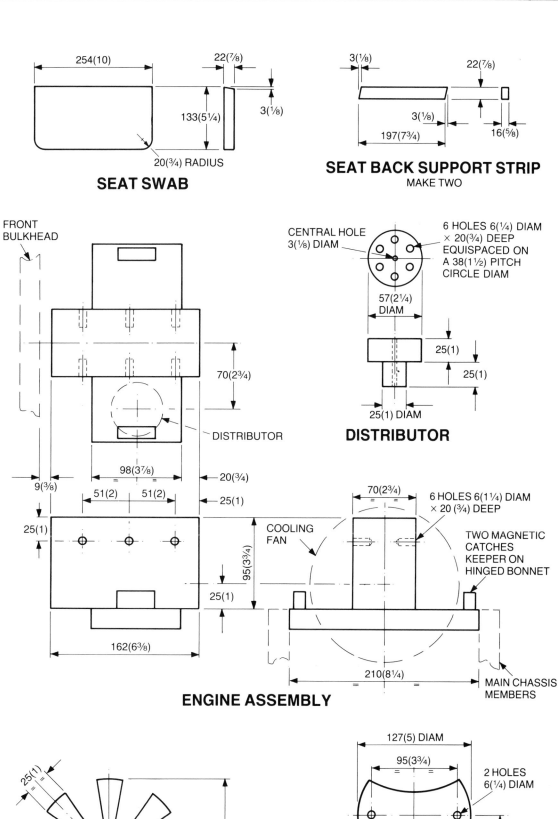

254(10)   22(⅞)

133(5¼)   3(⅛)

20(¾) RADIUS

SEAT SWAB

3(⅛)   22(⅞)

3(⅛)   16(⅝)

197(7¾)

SEAT BACK SUPPORT STRIP
MAKE TWO

FRONT BULKHEAD

CENTRAL HOLE 3(⅛) DIAM

6 HOLES 6(¼) DIAM × 20(¾) DEEP EQUISPACED ON A 38(1½) PITCH CIRCLE DIAM

57(2¼) DIAM

70(2¾)

DISTRIBUTOR

98(3⅞)   20(¾)

9(⅜)   51(2)   51(2)   25(1)

25(1)   25(1)

25(1) DIAM

DISTRIBUTOR

COOLING FAN

70(2¾)

6 HOLES 6(1¼) DIAM × 20(¾) DEEP

TWO MAGNETIC CATCHES KEEPER ON HINGED BONNET

95(3¾)

25(1)

162(6⅜)

210(8¼)

MAIN CHASSIS MEMBERS

ENGINE ASSEMBLY

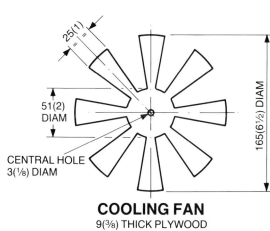

25(1)

51(2) DIAM

165(6½) DIAM

CENTRAL HOLE 3(⅛) DIAM

COOLING FAN
9(⅜) THICK PLYWOOD

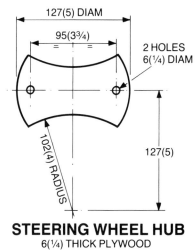

127(5) DIAM

95(3¾)

2 HOLES 6(¼) DIAM

102(4) RADIUS

127(5)

STEERING WHEEL HUB
6(¼) THICK PLYWOOD

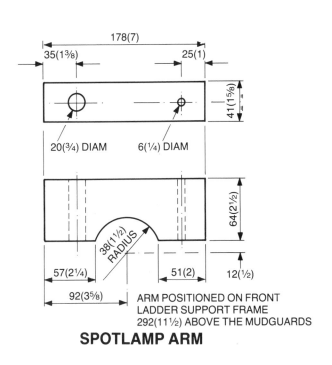

SPOTLAMP ARM

178(7)

35(1⅜)   25(1)

41(1⅝)

20(¾) DIAM   6(¼) DIAM

64(2½)

38(1½) RADIUS

57(2¼)   51(2)   12(½)

92(3⅝)

ARM POSITIONED ON FRONT
LADDER SUPPORT FRAME
292(11½) ABOVE THE MUDGUARDS

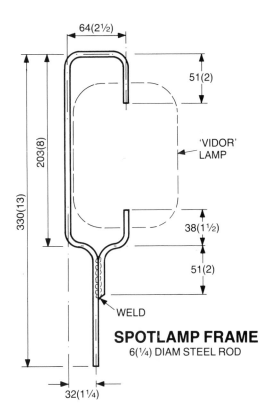

64(2½)

51(2)

203(8)

'VIDOR' LAMP

330(13)

38(1½)

51(2)

WELD

32(1¼)

SPOTLAMP FRAME
6(¼) DIAM STEEL ROD

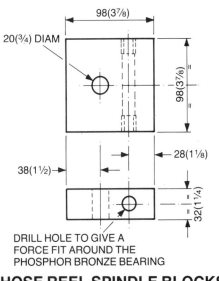

98(3⅞)

20(¾) DIAM

98(3⅞)

28(1⅛)

38(1½)

32(1¼)

DRILL HOLE TO GIVE A
FORCE FIT AROUND THE
PHOSPHOR BRONZE BEARING

HOSE REEL SPINDLE BLOCKS
MAKE TWO

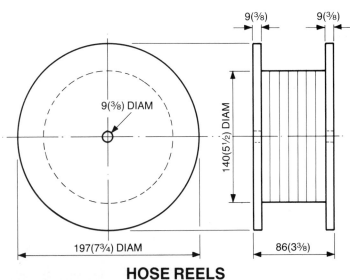

9(⅜)   9(⅜)

9(⅜) DIAM

140(5½) DIAM

197(7¾) DIAM   86(3⅜)

HOSE REELS
MAKE TWO

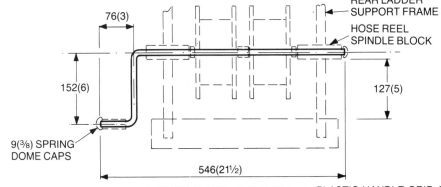

76(3)

REAR LADDER
SUPPORT FRAME

HOSE REEL
SPINDLE BLOCK

152(6)

127(5)

9(⅜) SPRING
DOME CAPS

546(21½)

HOSE REEL SPINDLE
9(⅜) DIAM STEEL ROD

PLASTIC HANDLE GRIP AND SPACERS,
FROM 9(⅜)I/D × 12(½)O/D TUBING:-
HANDLE – 57(2¼) LONG
CENTRE SPACER – 28(1⅛) LONG
OUTER SPACER – 12(½) LONG – 2 OFF

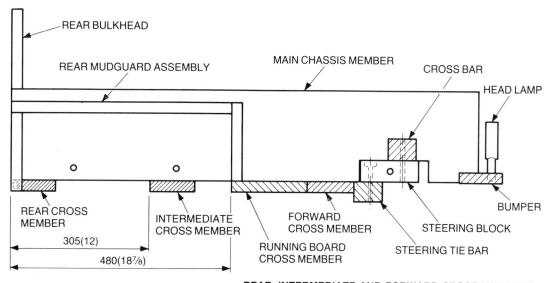

CHASSIS ASSEMBLY

REAR, INTERMEDIATE AND FORWARD CROSS MEMBERS
$254 \times 98 \times 22 (10 \times 3\frac{7}{8} \times \frac{7}{8})$
RUNNING BOARD CROSS MEMBER
$451 \times 168 \times 22 (17\frac{3}{4} \times 6\frac{5}{8} \times \frac{7}{8})$

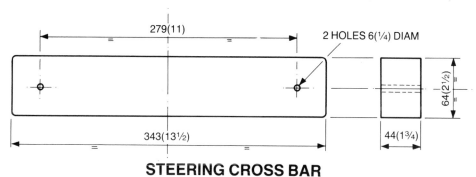

STEERING CROSS BAR

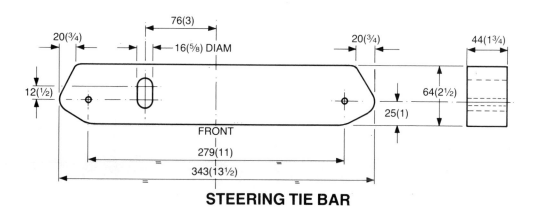

STEERING TIE BAR

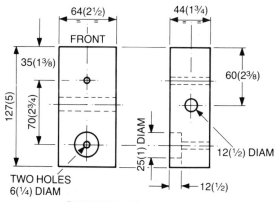

STEERING BLOCK
MAKE TWO

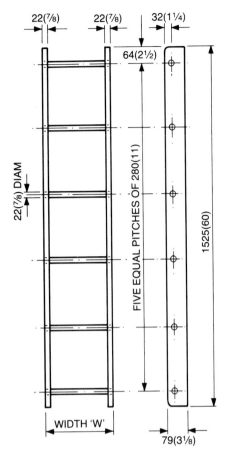

22(⅞)   22(⅞)   32(1¼)

64(2½)

22(⅞) DIAM

FIVE EQUAL PITCHES OF 280(11)

1525(60)

WIDTH 'W'

79(3⅛)

LADDERS

MAKE TWO, ONE WITH W = 248(9¾)
AND THE OTHER WITH W = 298(11¾)

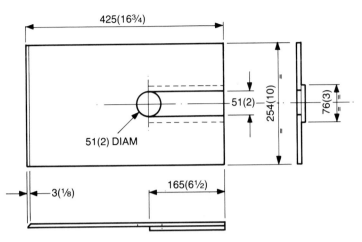

425(16¾)

254(10)

76(3)

51(2)

51(2) DIAM

3(⅛)

165(6½)

PUMP COMPARTMENT COVER

9(⅜) THICK PLYWOOD

PUMP COMPARTMENT FLOOR

381 × 127 × 9(15 × 5 × ⅜) THICK PLYWOOD
POSITIONED CENTRALLY AND SPANNING THE REAR AND
INTERMEDIATE CROSS MEMBER

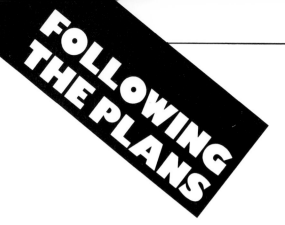

Depending on the complexity of each part to be made, the plan sheets show one, two or three views - usually top, front and side.

Various types of lines and symbols are used in these views to indicate different features. The example on this page will help you understand what they mean.

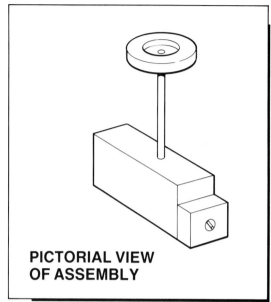

**PICTORIAL VIEW
OF ASSEMBLY**

DIMENSIONED PLAN VIEWS OF ASSEMBLY

SHORT DASHED LINES *indicate detail hidden in this view.*

A LONG DASHED LINE *is used to show position of adjacent parts.*

CHAIN DOTTED LINES *indicate the centre line of that part.*

DOUBLE EQUAL SIGNS *indicate symmetrical (equal) dimensions either side of the centre line.*

View on top of front view

HATCHING *is used here to show that the item is shown in cross section. Hatching is also used to highlight decorative features where appropriate*

SHORTENED DETAIL *to save space on the page.*

THICK LINES *are used to show outside edges.*

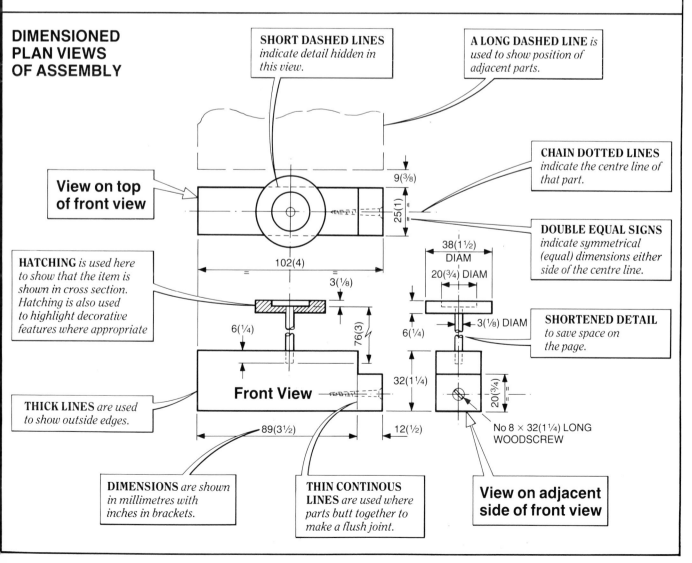

Front View

9(⅜)
25(1)
102(4)
3(⅛)
38(1½) DIAM
20(¾) DIAM
6(¼)
76(3)
6(¼)
3(⅛) DIAM
32(1¼)
89(3½)
12(½)
20(¾)
No 8 × 32(1¼) LONG WOODSCREW

DIMENSIONS *are shown in millimetres with inches in brackets.*

THIN CONTINOUS LINES *are used where parts butt together to make a flush joint.*

View on adjacent side of front view

Making a template

Drawing a squared grid over a picture and then copying it onto a larger or smaller grid is a very easy way of reproducing shapes to the size you want.

To make a template of a shape you wish to cut out of wood (e.g. the dragon's head for the Viking longboat), draw a grid on to a piece of card about the same size as the piece of wood you are going to use. Copy the shape given in the plans on to the larger grid using the squares to help you. Then cut out the shape and draw round it on to the wood.

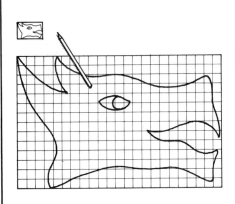

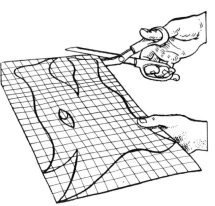

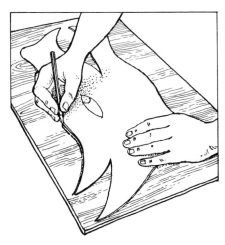

The halving joint is such a useful basic joint to learn. Once you have mastered the technique you can use it in a great number of projects.

Firstly mark out the width of the halving joint using a carpenter's square and a pencil (bottom left). If you prefer you can then scribble over the piece to be removed. You then use a marking gauge (left) to mark the depth of the halving joint. Trail the marking gauge at a 45° angle along the wood. The spike will leave a clear line for your saw and chisel to follow. Once the marking gauge has been set to half the width of the wood (hence the name 'halving joint') you do not need to re-set it for the other pieces of timber that will complete the joint.

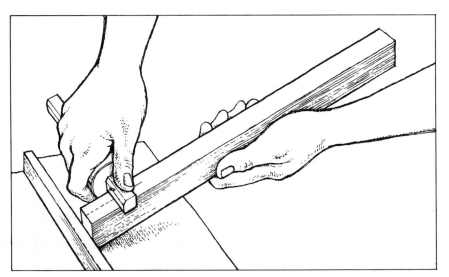

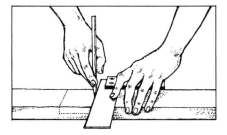

A sliding bevel gauge is an essential tool for marking out angled halving joints. Use a protractor to set the angle.

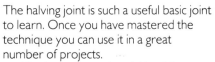

After marking out your joints and cuts in pencil and checking them, you achieve a much cleaner result by going over them with a marking knife. The knife cuts through the fibres of the wood and gives the saw teeth a line to follow.

Converting timber to useful lengths and widths is done with a panel saw (right). The best ones have wooden handles and taper ground backs and are very expensive, but you can buy a much cheaper tool with hardpoint teeth. Hardpoint teeth will stay sharp for longer than the conventional tooth saw, but when the saw begins to blunt you cannot have it re-sharpened.

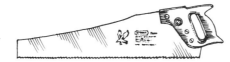

Tenon saws (right) get their name from the job they are usually used for – cutting tenons, which are the peg part of a mortice (the hole) and tenon joint. (These joints have not been used in this book.) The stiff metal back of this saw supports the blade so that it cuts accurately. The cheaper ones have a steel back, but the best have a substantial brass back. The brass gives weight to the tool and makes cutting a far easier task. Once again, tenon saws with hardpoint teeth are available.

An electric jigsaw (right) is often the DIY enthusiast's introduction to power sawing. It is quick and versatile, and there is a tremendous variety of blades available for cutting wood, metal, leather, plastics and so on, making it a jack-of-all trades.

When using a jigsaw to cut plywood, it is a good idea to use a metal-cutting blade which tends to file away, rather than cut the plywood and so is less likely to result in splinters. You can also tape over the back of the area to be sawn with masking tape to prevent this happening.

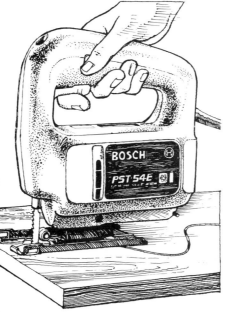

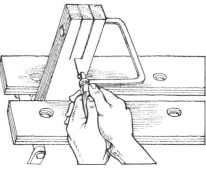

The coping saw (above) is undervalued today and much of its work is now done by the electric jigsaw (see below left). It can cut almost everything a jigsaw can – only slower! The blade can be rotated in the frame, so that it can cut awkward angles and remove fiddly waste sections.

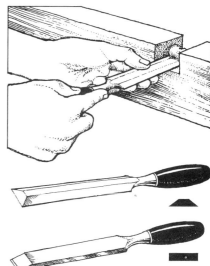

A good set of chisels is a must. The bevel-edged chisel (top) is probably the most useful, but if you need to cut fairly shallow mortice holes, then the firmer chisel is best (bottom).

A spokeshave (above) is used in the smoothing of all curved surfaces, and comes with either a flat or convex sole.

A good beech wood mallet is essential for striking the end of your chisel. Never, never use a hammer.

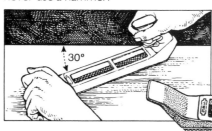

The surform has a set of fine teeth (resembling a cheese grater) which are capable of removing shavings from timber. Skewing the tool (by about 30°) as you use it allows you to remove shavings more rapidly than if you just work it backwards and forwards.

The success of any woodworking project will depend on how accurately you mark it out and this illustration shows how to mark out several pieces of timber identically by clamping them together. This is the technique to use for the see-saw stand, the slide framework and anywhere where repeated marking out of the same joints or cuts is needed. A variety of clamps are available from the traditional 'G' clamp (below) to the modern 'jet clamp' which has nylon heads that don't mark the wood.

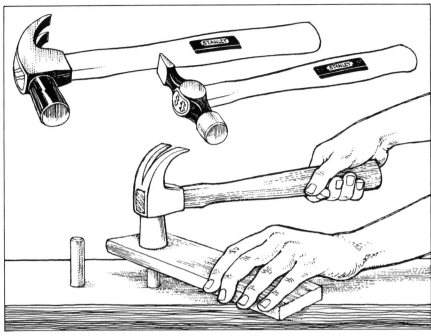

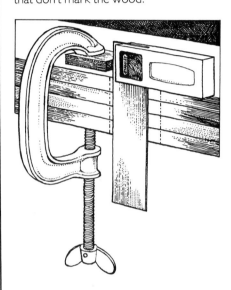

Webb straps are ideal for certain clamping jobs, e.g. clamping up the post van.

Don't compromise when you buy a hammer. There are some very cheap imports on the market which are extremely dangerous to use. The heads can work loose and can fracture. Hammer heads made by quality firms such as Stanley are all 'X-rayed' for flaws and are fitted to stay on the handles for life.

Illustrated are two different hammers: the left-hand one has a claw for extracting nails; the other is a lighter weight model for driving in panel pins.

Hammer heads will damage wood so protect the piece to be hammered by a scrap piece of wood. This is particularly important when driving dowel rods into holes, as shown here.

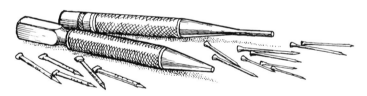

Nails and panel pins need to be driven below the surface of the wood so that they are secure and can't be seen. To

achieve this you need a nail or pin punch. The nail punch has a slightly concave end, while the pin punch has an elongated end.

Glue

A resin wood glue (such as Evostick Resin W) is the most popular kind of glue among woodwork enthusiasts as it is already mixed and comes in convenient containers. A water-resistant type for external use is available, but is not suitable for a real outdoor toy that has to withstand the elements day in, day out for years.

The 'one shot' glues, however, are really fully water-resistant and come under the brand name of Cascamite. These glues come in a powder form and have to be mixed with water when you are ready to 'glue-up'. This glue is suitable for all outdoor toys.

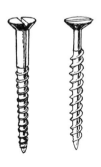

In addition to traditional woodscrews (left) you can now buy 'superscrews' (right) which have a different thread. These are particularly useful for plywood as they can be driven in more easily.

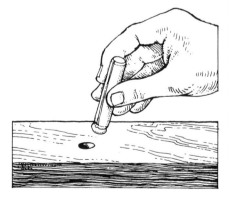

Dowel rods are sometimes oversize or even oval in section. Check for these faults before you buy. When fitting dowel rods into holes, chamfer off the ends to make the job easier.

Driving screws into wood is a basic operation for which, of course, a good screwdriver is required. Different-size screws need different drivers. The top one is the traditional type, but you can make substantial savings in effort by purchasing a Stanley 'Yankee' (bottom). These drivers have a spiral blade and when the handle is pumped, it drives the screw into the wood very quickly. Another great advantage is the different bits that are available for it.

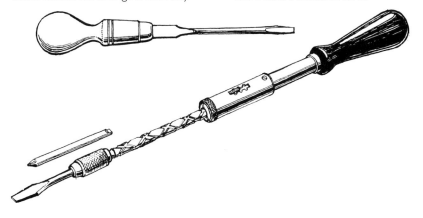

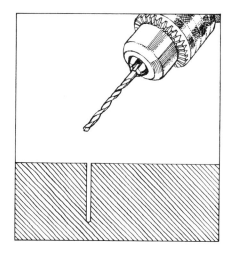

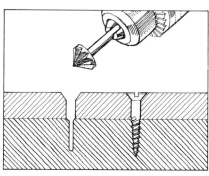

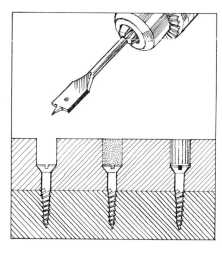

Electric drills do a great deal more than just bore holes as the attachments in any tool catalogue will show you. Most models now have two speeds: a low speed for drilling into brick and a high speed for boring into wood. You will need a variety of bits for the projects in this book and, of course, a chuck key to tighten them into the tool itself.

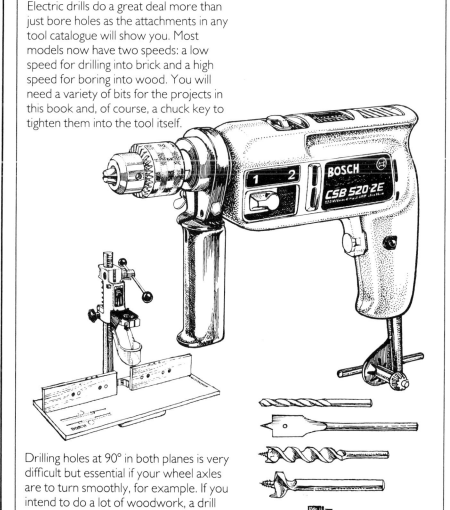

Drilling holes at 90° in both planes is very difficult but essential if your wheel axles are to turn smoothly, for example. If you intend to do a lot of woodwork, a drill stand is a very good investment as it enables you to drill at exactly the angle you require.

Screws cannot be cleanly driven into wood without a pilot hole being drilled first (top). The hole then has to be countersunk so that the screw head lies flush with the surface of the wood (centre). Sometimes it is helpful to counterbore a screw hole (bottom) – for example, when fixing two thick pieces of wood together so that you don't need to use an extremely long screw. This can be done quickly with a flat drill bit the size of the screw head concerned. However, flat bits have a tendency to bend. If you can afford it, buy a large wood-boring bit for this job which will last longer. Once drilled, the counterbored hole can be filled with stopping or dowel rod so that the screw head is completely hidden.

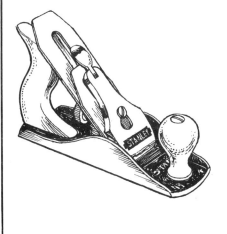

A smoothing plane (top) is an excellent investment and a good one will last a lifetime. The block plane (centre) is useful for trimming the end grain of legs, doors, etc. Plough planes (bottom) are designed to cut grooves or trenches in wood. They come with a range of cutters of different widths.

The electric plane (below) is ideal for converting sawn lumber to planed timber and can save quite a bit of money after the initial outlay. You may want to invest in a stand to hold the machine, leaving your hands free to manipulate the wood.

A piece of glasspaper wrapped around a cork block (below) is ideal for finishing off surfaces and ensuring they are completely smooth.

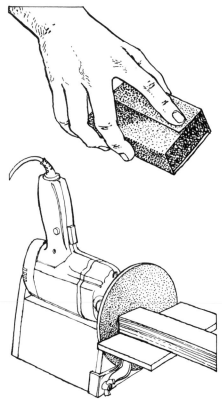

The end grain of timber is always difficult to finish well. An electric drill fitted with a sanding disc (above) is useful for this job.

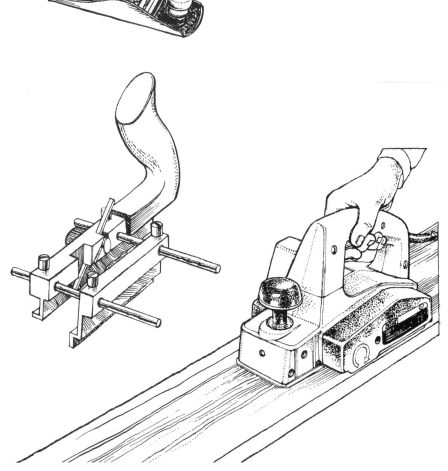

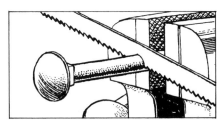

Perspex needs to be cut with a fine-toothed saw (panel or tenon). Mark on the perspex the line to follow using a felt-tip pen and then begin to saw across, keeping the saw at a very shallow angle. Make sure the saw is always in contact with two or three ridges at a time. Get an assistant to bend the cut section of the sheet down and away from the saw.

There are special packs of screws, washers and caps available for use with perspex (bottom right).

Hacksaws (top right) are essential for cutting off coach bolts and steel axle rods. Some very neat junior hacksaws, such as the one illustrated, are available.

The ends of steel axle rods need to be chamfered off before you can fit spring caps (centre right). This should be done with a smooth cut file. The spring cap can then be pushed on with the palm of your hand. On no account use a hammer to drive them on, otherwise you will damage them.

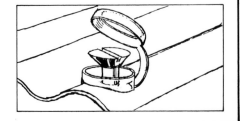

**By Peter Grimsdale
Director, The Swedish Finnish
Timber Council**

Virtually all of the projects featured in this book are made from Scandinavian softwoods. They are available from all timber merchants and DIY stores, easily worked and will last a lifetime outdoors if properly preservative-treated. As far as Sweden and Finland are concerned, their total export to Britain is in two softwood species: European redwood (sometimes called pine, deal or red deal, or, in the lower qualities, knotty pine) and European whitewood (sometimes called white deal, white pine or spruce). Either species is suitable for the projects in this book.

Buying softwood
Softwood is usually sold graded on the basis of freedom from knots and other natural features. As far as the home buyer is concerned this may not be a very helpful yardstick. The actual appearance of the timber is likely to be the most important consideration.

Our advice is to pick the timber you want. If your supplier will not let you see the timber you want to buy, then go elsewhere. Do not order timber by telephone where appearance is important.

Moisture content
Timber is a cellular material which will pick up and lose moisture depending on conditions. It is not sponge-like but if the timber is not seasoned properly in the first place or if timber is left uncovered then there is a good chance that it will be unsuitable for your use.

Timber can swell, shrink or split as a result of large changes in moisture content. If you buy wet timber and make one of the projects in this book out of it, then you will almost certainly have problems with shrinkage and distortion.

There are, however, several ways to minimise this problem. First, it is important for the timber to have been properly dried before arriving at your supplier's shop. Virtually all Swedish and Finnish timber is kiln-dried but not all timber from other countries is so check before you buy.

If the timber feels wet, or you can see that it has been kept outside unprotected, don't buy it. And, don't forget to put the timber under cover at home until you are ready to use it.

Sizes and lengths
Timber from European countries is sawn to metric sizes and cut to metric lengths. You may see timber displayed as 4 × 2in etc. but you can be fairly sure that it is in fact 100 × 50mm etc. as sawn. If the difference in size is important, for example when matching up with existing work, mention this to your supplier. Timber available for the DIY enthusiast ranges in thickness from 12mm to 75mm and in width from 25mm to 225mm. (These are all sawn sizes.)

For the DIY trade, merchants will often plane the timber for you. You will see this referred to as p.a.r. (planed all round) or p.s.e. (planed and square edged). If the timber has been planed then it will be 3mm to 5mm smaller than the sawn sizes. Not all suppliers plane to exactly the same size so if matching up is important stick to one source of supply.

Preservation
Many timber merchants now stock timber impregnated with a chemical preservative. This ensures durability and is vital where timber is to be used out of doors. If you want to use preservative-treated timber then check with your merchant first. He may have to order what you require. If the timber is to be in ground contact, for example the base of the swing, then it is essential for the wood to be properly impregnated by your supplier. The alternative is rotten timber after a year or two of use.

Of course, for less exposed conditions you can undertake the preservation yourself. Flood-coat the timber with a proprietary preservative and stand the end grain of the timber in a bucket of the preservative to soak in for a couple of hours. Wear proper protective clothing and gloves when working with preservatives, and work in a well ventilated place, preferably out of doors.

Do be aware that the decorative stains which are available on the market for staining your timber are *not* preservatives. Although they contain a fungicide to prevent mould growth on the timber surface they will not give adequate protection to the timber. Also, if you notch or drill the timber after

treatment you should then swab the timber exposed with more preservative. (Creosote is still a popular preservative but is best avoided for the toys in this book. It is oily and smelly and should only be used where there is no risk of contaminating clothing.)

Finishing timber
If the finished project is left out of doors for long and doesn't have a paint finish it will 'grey' under the sunlight. Many people use clear varnishes to try to prevent this but varnishes do not protect timber from the direct effects of sunlight. The timber degrades underneath the varnish which subsequently peels. Unless you are prepared to remove and re-coat the timber virtually every year, don't use clear varnishes on outdoor toys.

If you want to retain the natural colour of the wood, look for one of the modern exterior wood stains and buy one that is pigmented to match the colour of the timber. Decorative stains in a wide variety of colours have become very popular in recent years for use outside. The surface requires only a wash down and a re-application of the finish to maintain it. This should be carried out before the finish has lost all of its colour, usually in 3–5 years.

New paints
Until recently, the only external paints available for wood were the hard brittle paints which break down within about one year of application. Paint peeling off recently painted timber is a common sight in Britain.

The paint industry has at last brought out a range of opaque paints specially for use externally on timber. These paints cost a little more than the ordinary kind, but offer increased paint life (8–10 years has been reported) and simpler maintenance. Look for the words 'for use on exterior timber' or 'external quality' on paint cans.

A note from Richard Blizzard on plywood
I have found the best plywood to be Scandinavian as this is birch-faced and very high quality. Far Eastern plywoods are cheaper but tend to splinter easily. You pays your money and takes your choice!

INDEX

B
Bevel-edged chisel, 91
Bit, wood-boring, 93
Block plane, 94

C
Carpenter's square, 90
Castle, 52–63
Chisels, 91
Clamps, 92
Coping saw, 91

D
Deal, 95
Dowel rods, 92
Drills, electric, 93–94
Dump truck, 32, 34–36, 49

E
Eastern plywood, 95
Electric drills, 93–94
Electric plane, 94
European redwood, 95
European whitewood, 95

F
Fire engine, 64, 75–88
Firmer chisel, 91

G
Garden house, 49, 71–74
'G' clamp, 92
Glasspaper, 94
Glue, 92

H
Hacksaws, 94
Halving joint, 90
Hammers, 92

J
'Jet clamp,' 92
Jigsaw, electric, 91

M
Mail truck, 38–39, 41–42, 44
Mallet, 91
Market stall, 25–27, 33
Marking gauge, 90
Marking knife, 90
Materials used for projects, 95

N
Nail punch, 92
Nails, 92

P
Paint, 95
Panel pins, 92
Panel saw, 91
Periscope, 7–8
Perspex, cutting, 94
Pine, 95
Pin punch, 92
Planes, 94
Plans, following, 89
Plough planes, 94
Plywood, 95
Projects
    castle, 52–63
    dump truck, 32, 34–36, 49
    fire engine, 64, 75–88
    garden house, 49, 71–74
    mail truck, 38–39, 41–42, 44
    market stall, 25–27, 33
    periscope, 7–8
    see-saw, 21–23
    shovel loader, 43–44, 46–48,
        50–51
    slide, 17–20
    strength tester, 9–12
    swing, 13–16
    Trojan horse, 37, 64–69
    Viking longboat, 28–31

R
Resin wood glue, 92

T
Template, making a, 90
Tenon saws, 91
Timber
    buying, 95
    finishing, 94, 95
    marking out, 92
    moisture content of, 95
    preservation of, 95
Tools
    chisels, 91
    clamps, 92
    coping saw, 91

dowel rods, 92
electric drills, 93
electric jigsaw, 91
glasspaper, 94
glue, 92
hacksaw, 94
hammer, 92
mallet, 91
marking knife, 91
nails and panel pins, 92
panel saw, 91
planes, 94
sanding disc, 94
screws, 92–93
sliding bevel gauge, 90
spokeshave, 91
surform, 91
tenon saw, 91
webb straps, 92
Trojan horse, 37, 64–69

S
Sanding disc, 94
Scandinavian plywood, 95
Screwdrivers, 93
Screws, 92–93
See-saw, 21–23
Shovel loader, 43–44, 46–48,
    50–51
Slide, 17–20
Sliding bevel gauge, 90
Smooth cut file, 94
Smoothing plane, 94
Softwood, 95
Spokeshave, 91
Spruce, 95
Stains, 95
Strength tester, 9–12
'Superscrews', 92
Surform, 91
Swing, 13–16

V
Varnish, 95
Viking longboat, 28–31

W
Webb straps, 92
Woodscrews, 92